The Working Poet II

50 Writing Exercises
and a Poetry Anthology

First edition

ISBN: 978-1-59539-017-2
MAMMOTH books
is an imprint of
MAMMOTH press inc.
7 Juniata Street
DuBois, Pennsylvania 15801

www.mammothbooks.org

Cover design and typesetting by Enterline Design Services LLC.

Production by Offset Paperback Manufacturers, Inc.

The Working Poet II

50 Writing Exercises and a Poetry Anthology

EDITED BY

Scott Minar

MAMMOTH books
DuBois, Pennsylvania

CONTENTS

READING ANTHOLOGY: MAMMOTH BOOKS POETS

PREFACE

Welcome to *The Working Poet II: 50 Writing Exercises and a Poetry Anthology*, an updated edition of *The Working Poet*, first published in 2009. We are excited to announce that this Mammoth Books edition features a carefully crafted selection of exercises from the original edition, a new anthology of poems for class discussion and modeling, plus a new essay on apprenticeship by Edward Dougherty and a list of useful web sites for students of poetry and writing. We have worked hard to improve this edition, and we are proud to offer it to professors, teachers, workshop leaders, and individual writers as a resource. Our profound hope is that this book will be a useful complement to writing practice and instruction for years to come.

I am grateful to Tony Vallone, founder and editor of Mammoth Books, for reprinting such an impressive and stimulating set of poems from the authors on Mammoth's lists. The anthology of poems in this book reflects his excellent eye for poetry. I also wish to thank my fellow contributors from *The Working Poet* and the individual authors and Mammoth Books poets who have reprised some of their best work for our delight and inspiration. Each Mammoth Books author has selected her/his own poems for inclusion here, carefully choosing pieces that are the most useful to student writers for classroom or workshop use. These poems, however, will prove equally efficacious for individual writers in their own writing spaces and practices as well. I think the poets included here have done a wonderful job, and this book is considerably enhanced because of their thoughtfulness in choosing poems for the anthology. I wish new and familiar users of this book *Bon voyage!* Thanks to the dozens of nationally recognized and talented artists presented here, this is a journey well worth taking.

INTRODUCTION

My friend and former professor, David Heaton, told a funny story in graduate school. It goes like this: A graduate student has long admired the poet Wallace Stevens and decides one day to visit him. Traveling to Hartford, Connecticut where Stevens works in the insurance business, the student finds Stevens in his office and spends some time with him, asking all the questions one would want to ask the great poet. Upon leaving Stevens' office suite, the student notices the most junior agent, an intern sitting at the smallest desk right next to the door. The student stops and says to the intern, "My god, do you realize who you have in there?" The intern looks up, a little bored, and replies, "Let me tell you something. I write better insurance than that guy does." The graduate student walks away puzzled and forlorn.

I love this story for a number of reasons. The intern's implied assertion that the company knew very well who Wallace Stevens was and kept him around *because* he was famous is hilarious—especially with regard to the caricature of graduate students who probably tend to take things a little more seriously than they should. (In retrospect, I count myself among them.) That Stevens, or any accomplished poet, should have to work for a living is lampooned in this story too: of course he should; so should we all. It's humorous as well that Stevens is portrayed as not being very good at his job, at least as far as this upstart is concerned. Finally, I like the implication that work too has a value. Inspiration may be lovely, but it does not get the insurance written or the dishes done or the buildings raised (or razed). That takes another quality: a work ethic. I call this book *The Working Poet*, then, and dedicate it to the graduate student. And the intern. And, of course, to Stevens himself. All people who study poetry in depth know very well that it is, as the saying goes, 90% perspiration. The young intern may not have known it—but Stevens worked hard, very hard. You have to sit at your desk—at the coffee shop, in the bus station, at the airport, in the kitchen, on a box at work—and write. You have to write every day and dedicate your life to it. Whenever I see a wonderful poem, and I see many, I never see inspiration (though I know that it plays its part). Instead, I think of the hours and days, the weeks and the years a poet spent getting this work done. This book is intended to help guide students of poetry who would like to begin a journey down that road.

The Working Poet is an exercise book *and* a poetry anthology. The exercise portion has been designed to provide writers with a variety of methods, strategies, tricks, and ideas that engage active-learning strategies for poetry writing. There are many individual exercises here, as well as a number of exercises designed for a writing group. Of course, all of these individual exercises may be attempted by a group of writers in collaboration and consultation with one another. It is both in the nature of poetry writing and, I believe, in the skill of the contributors to this collection that both beginners and advanced writers may engage these exercises effectively and enjoyably. As a writing instructor, I have always adapted my approaches to the needs and qualities of my students or to the accommodation of my own desire for new perspectives. *The Working Poet* will prove useful both to teachers and students who follow the sequence provided here and to those who wish to simply "graze" through these exercises following their own inclinations and the path of a particular exercise that may catch their attention.

The anthology of poems by Mammoth Books authors that follows the exercises in *The Working Poet II* is a resource providing both materials for class discussions about poetry and models for student writers to follow. I tell my students never to begin drafting a poem unless they have read some great poetry first, and that the first and best exercise is to imitate the techniques and approaches found in a poem they really admire. I also tell them that no matter how hard they try, something original, something that is theirs alone, will always come through. Imitation is an imperfect exercise in this regard, and that is what makes it so valuable: that we may often learn from others and be "ourselves" at the same time. Poetry and poetic language are hermetic[1]: the energy of language passes from text to reader, from one writer to another stimulating the imagination and influencing thought.

---

1   Hermetics, an obscure term, refers here to the idea that words are magic, as opposed to a representation of it.

It has always been so. Although some psychologists will probably have a different view, this process seems magical to me. I like to believe that the authors whom I admire are urging me on. I go in the direction they have pointed out, yet I'm also on my own. In this collection of poems, I already have my favorites. I am confident that you will find yours too. The essay and list of useful web sites included in our appendices are also catalysts of thought and imagination. Such resources were irresistible as an aid and complement to this text's aims.

Finally, the idea here is to turn yourself into a *working poet* and to flourish because of your own efforts and through those of the teachers and fellow poets guiding you—the gifts of a strategy that can sustain one's writing for a lifetime.

The Working Poet II:

WRITING EXERCISES

JAN BEATTY

COMMENTS ON PLACE:
PUTTING YOUR FINGER ON IT

This is an exercise in "place" and an exercise in dreaming which enjambs the tangible and the surreal. I've used this exercise to get students to abandon habits of thinking and of structuring poems, so that they can lose their bearings and then regain them. This exercise is also meant to evoke a sense of play; to combine the literal with the wishful, dreaming voice; and to combine a sense of leaping with an unnatural, structured form and a time limitation. I like the idea of wonder running into time limits, not in a masochistic way, but in the way that it forces the writer to choose in that moment in time, what place appeals to her.

Place: Putting Your Finger On It

Begin with a globe or a world map. A globe is better, since it provides the sense of something more tangible, of three dimensions, and gives the students the immediate experience of spinning the globe and literally putting their finger on a place.

Narrative:
This is an exercise about locating yourself, your dreams, your accidental wishes, about constructing a house and world that is fanciful yet grounded. If you could build a house in your dreaming world, where would it be? What would be in it? Who would visit? Who would you become there, etc.?

1. Spin the globe, and then pick five places in the vicinity of where the world stops spinning. If you are in a group or class, name the places aloud, so that the group or class can be a part of this activity. Each person makes a list of her or his particular names. They can be any names, not necessarily the most flashy or seductive—so anything from

Intercourse, PA to the Caspian Sea. (Places can be cities, oceans, rivers, mountain ranges: anything seen on the globe).

2. Use this structure to work with:
    •   Begin the poem with the following line: "I will live in a house of _____."
    End the poem with the line: "You will know me by my _____."
    (They can complete the first and last lines in any way they like.)

    •   Use the five names of places from the globe in the poem.
    •   Use the names of three or four historical figures in the poem. These can be writers, artists, or anyone you might want to have in your dreaming world.
    •   Use the following words somewhere in your poem: "succulent, duct-tape, hilly-willy, purple, random, bookcase."

    * (Teachers: Choose any list of words that combines the playful, sensual, and concrete.)

3. Use this time limit and these guidelines:
    •   Write a poem of at least ten lines using all of the above ideas. Don't worry about line breaks, about crafting at this point, but pay attention to first and last lines and naming.
    •   Create a world that you would like to inhabit: don't worry about the "sense" of it—just connect the details and language.
    •   You have seven minutes.

4. Read your work aloud. (If you're in a group, just listen rather than offering comments or critique.)

Guidelines for later development:
    •   Return to this first draft and circle lines, images, ideas that are compelling to you.
    •   Using the circled sections, give yourself seven more minutes to

write whatever comes to mind—don't question what arises.

See what you have, and repeat this process until you have written all you can.

ROBIN BECKER

COMMENTS ON COMIC SIMILE
AND METAPHOR PORTRAIT

In this exercise, we use tropes (metaphor and simile) to create a comic portrait of someone we know. Characteristics of a person emerge as writers select and arrange images. The goals are to learn to vary sentence length and type, employ an opening and closing refrain, and choose words for their sounds and connotative associations as well as their denotative meanings.

Comic Simile and Metaphor Portrait

Write a poem, in complete sentences, that consists of ten-twelve lines, using only active verbs (emits, extracts, welcomes). Refrain from using the verb "to be" in any form. Open and close with the same line. Be sure to include an image from each of the required categories and place them in any order that suits your piece. The longest line may contain up to fifteen syllables.

Categories: Below are the eight suggested categories from which you will make up tropes. Formulate a category of your own, bringing the total to nine elements.

1. A food item (such as chocolate mousse)
2. An element of the natural world (such as peninsula)
3. The name of a particular job or profession (such as watchmaker)
4. A machine (such as coal stove)
5. An article of clothing (such as cashmere sweater)
6. A means of transportation (such as rowboat)
7. An animal (such as draft horse)
8. An article of furniture (such as ottoman)
9. Free Choice (such as telephone pole arms)

SAMPLE POEM

My Friend John

I think of John, with his head like a great peninsula,
bearing the twin ottomans of his shoulders.
With the kind eyes of a draft horse, he goes
about his work—chopping wood with his telephone pole arms.
Like a coal stove, aflame, his wide chest emits heat

but his hands, careful as a watchmaker's, extract
ice from the dog's paws. Soft as a cashmere sweater, his voice calls.
Sweet as chocolate mousse, his disposition welcomes.
Reliable as a lifeboat, his trustworthiness comforts us.
I think of John, with his head like a great peninsula.

—Robin Becker

ROBIN BECKER

COMMENTS ON NANTUCKET IMITATION

In this exercise, students use literal images in list form to guide the reader's eye in a particular direction. The selection and arrangement of detail challenges student writers to build a scene, image-by-image, and thereby create a particular atmosphere or tone. By repeating two adjectives twice (as Williams does with "white" and "glass") students work with single-word repetition. Students learn to manage loose couplets—with lines ranging from four to seven syllables—and to distinguish between complete sentences and incomplete fragments or phrases. Finally, drafting a ten-line imagist poem brings students "into conversation" with Williams and others whose poems depend on visual detail.

Nantucket Imitation

First, read William Carlos Williams' "Nantucket" carefully. After doing so, go to the activities below it. ("Nantucket" is easy to find on-line. Try poemhunter.com.)

1. Close your eyes and imagine a place out-of-doors that you know quite well. As you visualize this landscape or scene, position yourself as someone looking out at the place but not within the scene. In fact, no people are present and all activity has come to a standstill. (For example, the boat on the horizon rests in position.) Now, travel around the place, look at each element—discarded watering can, potting shed, heavy apple bough—and see it in relation to the other items in your scene.

2. List ten phrases (not complete sentences, not single words) that evoke this place. Use no abstractions (beauty, justice) and no evaluative adjectives (beautiful, majestic). Use concrete, descriptive words.

3. When you've made your list, go back and renumber your phrases, putting them in an order that appeals to you.

4. If working in a group, read your list, twice, to your partner. Your partner will paraphrase what she/he sees while you make notes on what needs clarification for your partner to see the scene as you intend. Exchange positions and respond to your partner's list. If you are not in a group, have a friend read your list to you and try your own paraphrase.

5. Discuss Williams' physical movement in space from far to near, his use of items in a list to show his scene, his choice of two adjectives. Try to identify the poem's tone.

Here is your assignment. Write a poem that includes the following: five couplets with no more than nine syllables per line; two repeated adjectives; movement in a clear "direction" in space; a collection of items that contributes to one tone—such as melancholic, celebratory, peaceful, agitated.

A few tips: Moving the reader's eye in space from far to near/near to far and low to high/high to low works best. Scanning across in a horizontal direction may become confusing.

CATHY SMITH BOWERS

COMMENTS ON TENSION IN POETRY

One of the most crucial elements of any sophisticated art is the element of tension. I define *tension* in two ways:

1. The pulling against each other of opposites, or
2. The upsetting of the reader's expectations.

A poet can enhance the tension in all four aspects of a poem—*feeling, story, language,* and *line.*

Tension in Poetry

Make a list of people you have conflicted feelings about. Beside each name write down a thing (song, piece of clothing, object, etc.) you associate with that person.

Now write a poem about that thing. This strategy will really help you zero in on the particular rather than floundering around in abstractions and generalities.

One way of making sure tension is present in the *feeling* and *story* aspects of the poem is to write about a person or place or thing you have conflicted, mixed, ambivalent or ambiguous feelings about. You can also then enhance the tension in the *language* aspect of a poem by using unpredictable or contradictory word choices and by shifting previous rhythms and syntax. You can use stanza and line enjambment (forcing the reader into the next line or stanza instead of allowing them to stop at those places) to enhance the tension in the *line* of the poem (My word for the way the poem is put on the page). Try to utilize all of these techniques in revising or shaping your poem. Be playful with this exercise; try to have fun using these techniques.

SAMPLE POEM

In my poem "Motherland" I write about a person I had/have conflicted feelings about. But since writing about a person is a huge task, I chose to write about a thing I associated with that person, in this case, my mother's weight, which she, herself, was obsessed with.

Mother Land

I pitied the other children
their skinny mothers. Nothing to burrow
when the church pew began to harden
like sugar-brittle or God. Their elbows
sharp as crags we climbed to the bluff
where Jimmy Adams took our dare
and jumped and never came up again. I pitied
them their mothers, all point and longitude,
tentative as sandbars the chain gang
dozed to stay the river banks. My mama

was a continent, terra softa
where she sprawled in her big chair
or across the bed when thunder ripped
the shingles and rain swelled the sills
like ripe earth. And there in the valleys
of blankets and pillows, each of us staked claim
to whatever fleshy region we had chosen to settle
while the storm spent itself. My sisters
nestling the soft slopes of her breasts, me floating
meridians of hip and thigh. My mama
was promised land and we, small redoubts
not even our father could penetrate, odd denizen

from that country of men we could see
mounting the horizon, their bright
flags flying, their cannons aimed.

—Cathy Smith Bowers

PAULA CLOSSON BUCK

COMMENTS ON LINE BYLINE:
FOUND NEWS POEM

I admire the ambition on the part of poets to write about the issues and events of their time, or about issues and events that might resonate with those of their own time. I also appreciate the difficulty of finding one's way into political material without becoming didactic or bombastic or just plain overwhelmed. This exercise offers a way of getting around such problems by privileging language and image over event and idea, at least temporarily. The result is typically a poem in which truth arrives as the found language rearranges itself (with the writer's help) on the page. What pleases me in the resulting poems is not only the kind of slippage and ellipsis that occurs but also the new commentary that emerges while the writer isn't thinking too hard about it.

I owe the inspiration for this exercise to two political found poems that I admire very much: John Gallaher's "Bomb Went Off," a poem created from a GOOGLE search using that phrase, and Matt Zambito's "Because the People of the World Want War," built out of phrases found, in sequence, in Richard Nixon's inaugural address.

Line Byline: Found News Poem

Materials:

1. The first few paragraphs of three or four articles from a current newspaper. (I print these out from *The New York Times* online, one page each, enlarging each article so that words and phrases can be easily cut out.)
2. A clean sheet of paper
3. Scissors and tape

Note: I have found that this exercise doesn't work as well when done on the computer. The specified materials (a novelty for young writers and a source of nostalgia for those not so young) help one to experience the physicality of the words as well as the ruptures and collisions that take place when they are moved in relation to one another.

Instructions:

Look over the photocopied paragraphs and headlines for phrases that strike you as interesting for any reason at all. Cut them out.

When you have assembled a lot of phrases, begin to build a poem out of them, laying them on your clean piece of paper, letting them delight and surprise you in the way they connect, grate on one another, shift meaning, create chasms and leap them. Don't think too hard. Rather, feel your way along and see what happens. I like the results best when I insist on full sentences, at least most of the time, to keep the poem from crossing over into chaos or nonsense.

SAMPLE POEM

For the poem that appears below, written in about forty minutes of class time, I used articles with the following headlines: "Many Children Lack Stability Long After Storm," "Attacks Traced to Two from Pakistan," "Soaring in Art, Museum Trips Over Finances," and "Auto Executives Face a Hard Sell on Capitol Hill." The fluctuations in font are an attempt to reproduce the cut and paste technique.

Fiscal Hawks

After more than three years of nomadic uncertainty,

blamed for   drug war

fed up   over fuel-efficiency   flunked out

in a suburb of Contemporary Art

        shrunk to about   face

We are not giving you the
advice to start smiling.

      A shy, artistic boy with a new mustache,

the one surviving   in the evacuee trailer

                   took much notice

as gruesome new evidence emerged

      a downturn and the realization

People sang as they sailed for the bottom line.

—Paula Closson Buck

NEIL CARPATHIOS

COMMENTS ON SUBVERTING THE ORDINARY: TIPS FOR TRANSFORMING THE FAMILIAR

In artistic endeavors such as poetry writing, one can't "learn" vision, but one can trigger the imagination in order to encourage fresh ways of seeing. For centuries, poets have attempted to make familiar subject matter less predictable, sometimes even turning to drugs, alcohol, or sleep deprivation in the attempt to rattle the brain from its slumber. Such extreme tactics are not necessary. The following exercise, in two parts, can activate the poet's internal "vision mechanism" and remind the poet of unexpected possibilities—in reality and in the mind.

Subverting the Ordinary: Tips for Transforming the Familiar

Part One: Inversion
By looking at things in a paradoxical way, by skewing vision to try to see objects and ideas outside of their logical frameworks, one can sometimes generate original descriptions and writing.

Try this: Describe something using an inversion of its most natural, expected meaning/connotation. In other words, describe your subject in *the opposite* way that one would expect it to be described. This imposes a certain freshness in dealing with an otherwise predictable subject. For instance, describe in detail

- the *violence* of a kiss
- the *beauty* of a can of garbage overflowing
- the *horror* of a sunset
- the *gentleness* of an act of murder
- the *comedy* of a dog seriously attacking a little boy
- the *hideousness* of a fully bloomed rose

... or any other subject that might work.

This can be done as a brief exercise (simple descriptions) or as an extended exercise with the poet writing an entire poem about the subject.

Here are two examples in which poets describe their subjects, whether purposely or not, in unpredictable, inverted ways. Consider these lines from Natalie Kenvin's poem "Farts":

Presumptuous, misbehaved stigmas,
They flare;
Breaking the rules of strict camouflage,
They hover askew in air
Like the wings of hunchbacked angels. . . .

In this poem, Kenvin clearly uses unique word choice. She describes the unpleasant subject of intestinal gas with pleasant, beautiful, even ethereal words: "hover askew" and "wings of hunchbacked angels." This treatment of her subject is the opposite of what is normally associated with the act of passing gas—namely, awful smells. Her poem, then, renders the subject in a fresh way, as if farts are delicate creatures of beauty! She has created an inversion.

For another example, consider James Wright's poem, "Saint Judas." In *Saint Judas*, both a fine sonnet and persona poem, Wright presents his historical subject in an unexpected light. He gives the reader a portrait that is tender, loving, even heroic—of one of the most notorious criminals in all of literature. He presents an imagined moment in the life of Judas in which Judas acts with kindness and compassion, indeed with near-saintliness as the title implies, which is contrary to the more commonly held "bad guy" version. Wright has inverted the traditionally viewed negative image of Christ's betrayer.

In both poems, the poets have turned their subjects upside down—with unusual word choice, imagery, or overall dramatic concept.

Part Two: Strangeness of Context
Similar to the inversion technique is strangeness of context. Sometimes by placing things in unexpected locations, one can intensify interest through

oddness of juxtaposition. For instance, one would not normally expect to see a door in a field. One also would not expect to hear a phone conversation about amputation while sitting to a delicious meal. Consider my own example:

The Door in the Field

Walking through a field
I came to a door
on the ground
some farmer must have lost
from the back of his pick up
on the way to the dump.
The hinges were rusty,
the blue wood splintered,
cracked.
It lay perfectly still,
the way wood does,
grass and dandelions shooting up
on all sides
from beneath it.
The doorknob was still attached
as if inviting me to twist
and pull. Daring me.
I wondered if it led
down a staircase to where
moles smoked cigars and played cards
hunched around tables,
or my father, wearing his body again
just for me,
waited to give a tour
using God's night vision goggles
which also work inside
Earth's dark.

Maybe the door jumped
from the farmer's pick up,
desperate to get back
to the little farm house
it was torn from,
crawled as far as it could
before dying, face up,
dirt gray Ohio sky
the last thing it saw.

—Neil Carpathios

Now experiment with strangeness of context. Take an item from the left column below and match it with a location in the right column. Then, write about this object in this unusual location. See where your imagination takes you. Why might the object be there? How did it get there? Does it cause the environment around it to change? Does anyone discover it? Etc. Turn your results into a poem.

martini glass	in the mailbox
watermelon	in the toilet stall
fingernail clippings	by the side of the road
Bible	under the covers in the bed

Note:
Some might argue that this two-part exercise encourages an artificial or contrived method of generating writing ideas. Obviously, genuine experience—deeply felt, lived, and explored—should be the primary source of a poet's material. However, the exercise can be useful to keep the mind flexible and open to wild possibility—and to remind oneself of the energy in oddness, even if self- imposed in the form of exercises. For example, my poem "The Door in the Field" was sparked while trying the strangeness of context technique described above. What started as an exercise describing an object in an unusual location, led to a deeply felt and unexpected reunion

with my dead father. As I visualized a door lying on the ground, I quickly knew that I would open the door; I did not, however, know that my father would be waiting for me down there.

ELIZABETH DODD

COMMENTS ON THE EKPHRASTIC POEM

When I first began teaching poetry writing as a graduate student in my early twenties, I always brought students to the art museum on campus, which was only a few minutes' walk from the building I taught in. Some years later, when I landed a teaching position at a campus that had no art museum, I realized what that loss meant. It's possible to achieve some of the assignment goals through other means—in a high-tech classroom, one has instant access to images of the world's great artworks, from all ages. Or, to get the field trip experience, one can go to the library and introduce students to the oversized volumes filled with reproductions. But actually taking students to a museum is better, if at all possible: some say afterwards that they've never been to an art museum before, and they love it. The institutional echo and hush, the tall ceilings and indirect light, the freedom after the tour is over to move about and then stop, spend long minutes before whatever most insistently catches their attention–these are all marvelous "pre-writing" experiences.

I use this assignment in a beginning poetry writing class that enrolls students from all over the campus—majors from English to Agricultural Economics, and a large number in Education, too. I like the way we're all newcomers to the material here—I try to schedule the visit when a new exhibit has just opened, so that the experience of *seeing* is equally fresh for them all (the English majors have no advantage here). Our museum staff is extremely helpful—we often are able to schedule a tour with a staff member or docent (allowing me to be a newcomer, too). If this isn't possible, I make a visit before class to learn something about the featured artists and get a sense of how to talk about the work suggestively.

Frequently, the very best poems of the term emerge from this assignment, full of vitality and surprise. For many students, the concept of evoking instead of explaining finally makes sense. They come to see language as an experiential force, not merely a reportorial one. Those are some of the exercise's primary goals, along with practice using imagery and figurative language. But less concretely, I want students to first *experience* aesthetically, and then *create* an experience themselves. This shift—from a position of audience to authorship, triggered by something from outside preexisting experience—can be transformative for beginning poets.

We make a return trip to the museum for workshop discussions of the poems, and each student reads her or his draft while we gather around the piece that inspired it. Occasionally, the poems they write are nearly incomprehensible without the artwork to illustrate it, and this allows us to talk about what makes a poem independent, how allusion functions, and similar matters. Nearly invariably, I find that after our museum discussions, the level of sophistication and resourcefulness in class discussions rises. The students are proud of their ekphrastic poems; they see them as significant steps in their entrance into poetry, and I do, too.

Ekphrastic Poem

Choose one piece—painting, sculpture, photograph—that seems to *speak to you*. (Or, put another way, let one of the pieces choose *you*!) Spend some quality time with your chosen artwork—looking, thinking, exploring how it makes you feel. You'll want to go prepared to take notes, do some free-writing, etc. Take a pencil; it's not considered good form to take an ink pen into a museum gallery.

As you examine your chosen artwork, think about how it is expressive (how it does that speaking to you). What kinds of color are used—bold colors, pastels, graphite? What kind of texture does it seem to have—fine lines, rough brush strokes? What medium has the artist used—clay, oil, collage, mixed media? If it's a sculpture, how does it use shape and texture? What happens as you circle it, see it from a different angle?

How do these various techniques create the mood you *feel* when you gaze at the work?

Write a poem based on the visual artwork. Your poem is a kind of interpretation, or enactment, of the artwork of your choice.

A visual artist establishes mood through color, line, texture. You'll rely on language, using words not only for literal description of what you see, but to evoke the feelings you experience while looking. Think of the sound of your words, the connotative power they carry.

Try any of these approaches:

Write a persona poem in the voice of an object, animal, or a person in the painting. What kind of voice will this speaker have? What kind of lineation—long or short, enjambed or endstopped? How do those lineation choices echo or mimic the visual technique you see?

You might describe the piece in an extended metaphor, or a series of different metaphors. If a painting is a visual experience, what happens if you imagine it as something auditory? If you're looking at a piece that is abstract, nonrepresentational, what happens if you decide to tell a story based on the patterns of feeling it evokes in you?

Imagine the artist working; you might imagine *yourself* as the artist working. What other information might help you "become" that other person? Read the artist's biographical information available at the museum, or if there is an "artist's statement," read that carefully. Is there any language she or he uses that you'd like to incorporate into your poem?

Imagine yourself entering the world of the painting or picture. Try standing on the opposite side of the room and walk steadily toward it: how does your changing position affect your feeling about the piece? How does it change what you actually see? Can you imagine leaving the museum hall altogether and stepping into the frame?

Find some poems that are written in response to paintings, sculptures, or photographs. Think about the various ways these poems respond to the art: How does a poet not merely describe looking at the painting, sculpture, or photograph, but make the reader feel she or he is looking at it, too? X.J. Kennedy says of Marcel Duchamp's "Nude Descending a Staircase," the image is a "One-woman waterfall," providing a metaphoric comparison for the cubist arrangement of the human figure going downstairs. You could imagine your poem being in a kind of dialogue with the sculpture or painting.

Remember, you are using language as an artistic medium, making the same kinds of decisions about word choice, rhythms, or sounds as a painter would make about colors, kind of paint, brush strokes. Content is only the first step—what you do with the content is where the real power lies.

EDWARD A. DOUGHERTY

COMMENTS ON ELECTRIC TITLES

When we shuffled our feet on carpets and shocked someone, we didn't need to actually touch for the electricity to be delivered. That is the arc of a good title: a jolt of energy built up in both the words of the title and the body of the poem. To work with this, we sometimes have to move in several directions. This exercise has three parts to help you learn how to explore the words of the title itself, how to name a draft of a poem, and how to start with a title.

Electric Titles

Shuffling Our Feet: Without reading the poems themselves, scan the names of the anthology poems in this book and choose 5-7 that stand out for you. Now separate the ones that connect to your own experience—ones that refer to places you've lived, for example, or events you know about. What's going on in the language of the remaining examples? Is there an image? A metaphor? Does it make a statement or raise a question? Look at the kinds of words the writer chose. For example, does the title focus on a verb and thus an action?

Copy out three that are doing different things and for each, imitate the language and dynamic to create three titles to poems you haven't written. You should have nine titles.

Extending Our Finger: In addition to imitating the style of others' titles, we can think of other ways to get poems started. (1) Make a list of unusual words or brief phrases which you find interesting, either because of their sound or their meaning. Strive for 10 or so. Delve into a wide range of your interests: gardening, science, gaming, sports, etc. My list includes "pyroplasticity," "gentrification," "rotator cuff," and "Downward Dog." Notice how the image and meaning begin making their own suggestions; now begin drafting, spinning off these suggestions, without using the word or explaining its meaning. If you get stuck, return to the originating image and spin in a different direction. (2) Painters often create titles for an image, a single portrait that needs to suggest the larger narrative or emotion. We can imitate their methods when making our titles. If they are merely descriptive, like "Landscape with Horses," and you look at the image and see, well a bunch of thoroughbreds out in a meadow, how much energy—delight, intrigue, mystery—is released? There needs to be something more, which I can feel when Magritte called a painting of a cello "A Little of the Bandits' Soul." Scan art books for good titles, copying out the most energetic, and imitate them as in #1 above.

Drawing out the Body: Take a draft of a poem of yours that either has no name or a title you're unsatisfied with. For "spark," find a point of contact (or a better point of contact) between the poem and the title (or potential title)—that's why lightning rods attract the electrical charge. Locate the most important moments in the poem. Underline the phrases you think are best and most central to what the poem is doing. Put a star by the images that are strongest. Now use them to create your title, but instead of naming them, take a phrase and sharpen it. If the image you starred is "the moonlight/shatters on the snow" you could simply name that image as your title "Moonlight on Snow" and so draw readers' attention to that section of the poem. Attentive readers will ask themselves how the image relates to the other aspects of the piece. You could also use the word "Shattered"—which not only achieves the same effects as the descriptive title but suggests an emotional state as well. Now you could also sharpen the metaphor a bit, elongating the gap between the image and the idea, and title the piece "Night of Broken Glass," which now adds the historical reference to the terrible events called *Kristallnacht* (literally "Crystal Night" but called the Night of Broken Glass) that took place in November of 1938 marking the outset of the Nazi's violence against the Jews. For your own poem, create three titles: a descriptive one from the central image or phrase, one that also has greater emotional connotations, and one that works harder metaphorically. Measure each not only against the poem itself, but against what you've discovered from doing the previous two title exercises.

JOHN GALLAHER

COMMENTS ON WORDS AND PICTURE

The goal of this exercise is to practice visualizing something specific that you must approach from out of a closed set of "accidental" words, approximating the spirit or tone of a picture or scene without trying to (or being able to) be simply descriptive.

Usually, when we're asked to imagine something, we move to story: what are the people doing? How did they get here? These are perfectly fine and generative ways to use pictures, but they tend to lead us into narrative as well as into our own ability to imagine. This exercise forces us to move from a generative imagination to an orchestrating imagination. The resulting poem is "formal" in that it is derived from a set of rules, but it doesn't have the outward signs of form. One could think of it as "Generative Form."

One can learn several things from writing in this manner. One is that "Form" doesn't have to simply refer to the way poems look on the page. As well, from this, one can practice generating images that, using found or accidental language, force one out of one's usual method of putting words together.

Words and Picture

For this exercise, you will need a newspaper—hopefully, a university or local free newspaper. Though any paper will work, university or local papers often have a wider range of tones to their language, as well as more mundane or local-interest pictures.

There will be a picture on the front of the paper. That is the vision (scene, whatever) for you to keep in mind.

Write a poem using only words found on the front page of the paper. Keep in mind the scene from the picture, but use NO words directly from the story or headline linked specifically with that picture. Approach this exercise however you wish (as play, or with a strong emotion). And remember, when writing this, to keep yourself open to the range of tangents and possibility for reference the available language allows.

The poem you produce could be anything from a language-oriented experiment in non-sequiters, to a seemingly biographical or autobiographical narrative. Often the poem will fail as a unity, but you might be left with a couple lines that are quite good that you can use for something else in the future.

MICHAEL GILLS

COMMENTS ON RISING EARLY

This exercise is why, I believe, my best mentors have always taught me to rise early—be near the dream consciousness.

Rising Early

This exercise should be conducted as follows. The student poet is asked to rise early—say 4:30, walk outside and register the strangeness of the world seen from the perspective nearest one's dream state. Then, with such material as one can discern from the dark under the night sky, walk back into the house and write exactly what one saw without editing. Later the same day, return to the work and make revisions. The resulting work is often surprising. At 4:30, one's inner censor is most often switched off—we are unafraid of making fools of ourselves. Likewise, in the hard light of the afternoon, revisions come easily, though the key is not to lose the rawness of the original experience.

SAMPLE POEM

First Frost
—for M.W.T.

If you own hogs in Utah
they're safe for the slaughter.
I'm maybe the first to know
barefoot in my underwear
dragging the thirty-foot tarp
over the headhigh
Big Boys, Mars
a fat-pumpkin, shines just north
of the bull's red eye--

what hunter hell-bent across
October sky? Glinting, yes, blond assassin, maybe
you show off
on a blade of dying grass.
My mother's father was one-legged,
hopped under the Hunter's Moon,
his shadow hump-backed
between me and the frosty well house.
I fight the urge
to laugh loud like him,
fling goddamns into the blue blank sky,
tarp strung tight over six-foot stakes
secure above our summer-green tomatoes
hard, the perfect size of fists.

—Michael Gills

MELANIE GREENHOUSE

COMMENTS ON DEEP IMPRESSIONS

I teach a weekly poetry seminar at an assisted living community for residents who range in age from their 70's to 90's. While many are fans of poetry (mostly traditional), none had ever attempted to write poems of their own. What I like about the following exercise is that the participants, at first, did not consider their personal experiences worthy of poetic material. It was gratifying to see how pleased they were with the results when given the benefits of line breaks and other poetic devices. What the exercise accomplishes is a renewed enthusiasm for language, a sense of the individual's potential for creativity, and a means of recording for posterity moments that would otherwise be lost. If I gave this exercise to younger writers, I would simply use the same methods, but add the student poem samples and ask the workshop members to contribute from their own perspectives or to imagine themselves, as an exercise, in the place of the older writers then write from that imaginary perspective.

Deep Impressions

As a warm-up, read and discuss familiar classical poems by Whitman, Dickinson, Longfellow, Browning, Whittier, and Frost—make note of the imagery, rhyme, rhythm, and meter in their works.

Next, read and discuss a variety of contemporary poets, with an emphasis on those who have written well into their senior years—Mary Oliver, Galway Kinnell, Donald Hall, Stanley Kunitz, Gerald Stern, Philip Levine, and Virginia Hamilton Adair. In the discussion, pay attention to simile, metaphor, alliteration, onomatopoeia, and sensory images in the work contemporary poets.

Finally, think about events from the deep past that left permanent impressions on you. Discuss why these events are imprinted in our memories. Then record the events either through dictation or using some of the poetic devices covered in previous sessions.

MICHAEL HETTICH

COMMENTS ON TRANSLATION INTO ORIGINAL POETRY

I use a version of the three-part exercise outlined below in virtually all of my creative writing classes. The students enjoy it a great deal, as it gives them a sense of empowerment and freedom—as well as a greater sense of the shapes and weights of words. Since virtually all of my students are bilingual, the first step of this process allows students to discuss various translation choices in a way that is valuable on both the conceptual and the linguistic level. In the rare cases in which I have had only a few bilingual students, I have made the translation groups larger, and I have asked the monolingual students to transform the rough translation into something that sings.

Note: For this exercise, the Vallejo poem and the Justice poem are both readily available on the Internet. I copy the Bly version from my old copy of *Neruda and Vallejo: Selected Poems.*

Translation into Original Poetry: An Exercise in Making It New

1. Sit in groups of three (or two or four, depending on skills and class size), and give them each Cesar Vallejo's "Piedra Negra Sobre una Piedre Blanca." Next, make a group translation of the poem—move fairly quickly but discuss those words and phrases that give you problems and/or may be interpreted a number of ways. This takes between fifteen to twenty minutes in most cases. Then take this literal (and rough) "translation" and start to focus and tighten the language so that it begins to read like a real poem in English. Provide enough time with this part of the exercise to finish the first stanza and perhaps a little more. But really we're just aiming for a sense of how a literal "translation" is turned into something actually worth reading.

2. After each group reads what they've come up with, both the literal (first) and then the literary, discuss tense, word choice (is it a rainy day or a

stormy one?), conception, etc. Literary versions are sometimes quite free in their interpretations—more like versions than translations. Talk about this too (it leads to interesting discussions).

3. I hand out Bly's and Knoepfle's translation, "Black Stone Lying on a White Stone," and let the students discuss it freely, which they inevitably do with great energy. In most cases some of us may be indignant at some of Bly/Knoepfle's choices—which gives us the opportunity to work on a fully-realized version, and, further, try our hands at translation in general. At this point, we have recognized the creative energy involved in generating literary translation. Use other available poems here if necessary or desirable.

    (Sometimes we stop here for a few minutes and examine one or two student poems we've already critiqued during the semester, to see whether some of the techniques we used in developing a literary translation from a literal one might solve some of the textual and/or conceptual dilemmas evident in those poems.)

4. Next I hand out copies of Donald Justice's "Variations on a Text by Vallejo," and read the poem aloud. Justice employs the Vallejo poem to make something original and entirely his while clearly drawing from its model. We see how this level of "translation," this imitation, simultaneously creates a conversation with the original and something new. Vallejo's conceptual sensibility is made graceful and "cooked" by Justice's formal sensibility. It is also possible to find other poems that demonstrate these features.

5. Finally, write imitations of any three of five poems provided to the group at this point (I use different poems each time), and try to respond to the original the way Justice responds to Vallejo—that is, to echo (and even repeat) certain key lines, but to attempt to create something entirely your own. (This, to my mind, is different from what Lowell did in *Imitations*, which seem to me to be simply loose translations.)

ANDREA HOLLANDER

COMMENTS ON THE MIRROR POEM

All poems are journeys. The journey of a mirror poem may seem at first to be circular, beginning and ending at the same place, but it is the texture of the journey, no matter its duration or destination, that makes such a journey deep and memorable.

Trying to write a mirror poem forces the poet to deal with the formal challenges of syntax and lineation. In my nearly twenty years of teaching poetry writing, I've found this exercise to work better than any other to compel poets to focus not only on a poem's content (its message or story or revelation) but very judiciously on its form, the impact of its form on the content, and the way such form interacts with the poem's content to enrich meaning.

A further benefit of the mirror poem is the number of discoveries made during the process of revision. No matter the length of the poem, no matter its subject, we try to craft our poems to use the fewest number of exactly right words to convey the deepest truths. During the work involved in shaping a mirror poem, the poet must continually alter the diction and the syntax (in both halves of the poem) in order to maintain the mirroring effect. Doing so demands rethinking the nature of syntax, sentence, line, stanza, diction, and parts of speech—all the characteristics of and opportunities afforded by language—sometimes discarding one strategy and discovering another.

Certainly the mirror poem is first of all an exercise. And with all exercises, the writer should not assume that the crafted result will automatically be a "real" poem. When the practicing poet cannot spin the exercise into gold, he or she will nevertheless find that subsequent poem drafts of any poem will have benefited from the attention paid to the formal challenges introduced here.

The Mirror Poem

Write a poem of at least twenty lines that takes the form of a mirror—a poem whose second half repeats its first half pretty much line by line but in reverse order. Resist the temptation to end-stop every line, and use enjambment as often as possible. As you shape the poem, you may vary the punctuation so as to alter the meanings of words used in the first half of the poem (*Some mornings we take walks* may become *some mornings. We take walks*). Take advantage of the slight alterations afforded by the difference between singular and plural parts of speech (The word *peach* in the first half may be changed to *peaches* in the second.). You may even add or remove some words or exchange an original word from the first half with a pure rhyme of that word in the second (*blows* may become *close*). If the lines of the first half appear this way,

Roses fell apart when she touched them,
no matter their age—or hers.
Men had come but always left

they may appear much different when mirrored in the poem's second (mirror) half:

Men came, but always left,
no matter their age. Her
roses fell apart. When she touched them

Notice here how the word *their* takes different antecedents in the two examples above. In the mirrored second half, the pronoun refers to the *men*, while in the first it had indicated the *roses*. Also in this example's mirrored section, the word *touched* may now refer to the men or the roses (depending upon the next line, which I did not provide here).

SAMPLE POEM

At Mt. Lebanon Cemetery

At Mt. Lebanon Cemetery snow
covered the stones. Footprints
told their familiar story over and over.

This afternoon we stood
in half circles holding hands
like strings of paper silhouettes unfolded.

In the parking lot, cars would come and go,
unsettling the melting snow that puddles now.
Over the newest graves
the earth, too, inches down.

I'll plant daffodils beside her stone.
That way I'll know
something will bloom each March
when no one kneels at her bones.

When no one kneels
will something bloom? Each March
I will know.
And daffodils too will die beside her stone.

Today the earth inches down
over the newest graves –
unsettling. Melted snow puddles now.
In the parking lot, cars come and go,

dark silhouettes unfolding.
In half circles holding hands
we stood this afternoon,

our familiar story over and over
covering the stones, our footprints,
the cemetery, the snow.

—Andrea Hollander

RICHARD JACKSON

COMMENTS ON THE TOP TEN LIST

This is an exercise aimed at getting you away from what Richard Hugo calls the "triggering subject" by forcing you to associate and connect a number of diverse elements. Samuel Johnson once described John Donne's poetry as "disparate images by violence yoked together." Your task is to make the disparate elements listed below yoked together in a seamless, non-violent manner!

The Top Ten List

Write a poem that starts with the "trigger" of a personal situation, but include the elements below. The point is to make you move away from the merely personal and solipsistic into larger contexts. Do not try to jam the items all together in a short space—extend them out; this is generally meant for a poem of 25 or more lines. No two items can be related in ways they usually might be.

1. A piece of fruit or vegetable
2. A window, door, portal or some such opening—a cave or arch is also okay
3. A machine or mechanical device
4. A famous person, real or fictional (from history, science, etc—not 20th century)
5. An exotic place
6. Something from science—a theory, principle, name, or idea like gravity
7. A means of transportation
8. A part of the body
9. An item, saying, event etc from another culture
10. An idea from philosophy or religion, or some such belief system

Of course you can keep modifying this exercise by changing the items on the list—just keep them disparate.

RICHARD JACKSON

COMMENTS ON THE FOURFOLD

Martin Heidegger, a modern philosopher and poetic critic, says in his essay "The Thing" that for the poet to get a sense of the real, he or she has to relate four things to any crucial physical object in the poem:

- *Earth:* the relation to the physical, changeable nature of things, the muck of experience, the particulars
- *Sky:* the sense of seasons, of larger patterns that seem to occur from the perspective of the sky, the sense of the weather, of what's happening just over the horizon
- *Divinity/Heavens:* the sense of the absent, the possible, of what might change things, the unreachable, but also a sense of the mystery of things
- *Mortals:* the sense of the mortality, the end of things, how and why things are used, defined, appreciated, culturized

This is Heidegger's way of showing how everything is connected. He has a dense, confusing, but poetic way of speaking. He's trying to get at the combination of presence and absence, actual and possible that we need in order to define our realities, that we need to determine what's at stake for us.

The Fourfold

The exercise is to take an object and describe it fully: the physical description and stories behind it, its origins and future. You should start with the physical description, and then begin associating rapidly to the object's origins and then the stories behind it: this associative process also serves to start you thinking generally about all that lies behind the immediately visible world, and so is a good exercise for the imagination. Everything becomes a story, a myth, one of the very origins of poetry.

* Some examples can be found in poems by Charles Simic, Vasko Popa, Gerald Stern, Anna Akhmatova, Miroslav Holub, and others. (An associated exercise is to write a creation story—to create a completely fictional myth about how something originated.)

MIKE JAMES

COMMENTS ON THE STAND-UP POEM

Most students believe writing a poem is all seriousness. We are normally taught to see a poet as a romantic truth teller, rather than as an entertainer. This exercise is designed to show that those two roles are not mutually exclusive.

The Stand-Up Poem

Begin with a discussion of comedians and the ways in which comedy serves to break down barriers. Include in the discussion the truths found in humor.

Next, talk about the ways some poets use humor and/or absurd situations as a technique. Poets who are sometimes fond of these techniques include Frank O'Hara, James Tate, Bill Knott, Charles Simic, Billy Collins, and Edward Field. A selection of poems from the poets chosen for the discussion should provide different examples of how an absurd line, concept, or situation can be used to develop an alternative logic and even a parallel universe.

Finally, try this assignment. Begin a poem with the most absurd line imaginable and follow it to its logical conclusion. An example might be something like, "If we always ran backwards would the world look the same?"

Make sure to focus more on the process rather than the end result. The purpose of this exercise is to not only get us to think differently about what a poem is, but also to provide a level of comfort with humor as a writing tool. If we are comfortable with humor, we are less likely to discount good ideas as they appear.

SAMPLE POEM

Necessary Fictions

The invention of soft-serve ice cream
Would have changed the cavemen
And all those paintings they left us

And who would want that

Those paintings are wonderful
Each one like the work
Of a gifted child

It's probably not right to call the work
Of pre-literate people childish
But they will never read this

Those figurative paintings
As basic as black

The cavemen drew the eternals
Deer, fire, funerals
A trio that always goes together

—Mike James

ILYA KAMINSKY

COMMENTS ON CORRESPONDENCE
AND INCANTATION

Anna Akhmatova once coined a term "correspondences in the air"—
that is, moments where authors of different geographical and historical
circumstances, languages, and traditions, seem to address each other in
their works. Such "correspondences in the air" abound in Twentieth Century
poetry as they do in any century. Perhaps the most important lesson we
can glean from these correspondences is how necessary it is for poets to
dialogue, to return to their poetic origins in order to create something new.
After all, the word "originality" in English has its roots in "origin." Or, as
American poet Frank Bidart suggests, we fill pre-existing forms, and in
filling them we change them, and are ourselves changed.

Let's consider one such set of "correspondences" by going back to
Ecclesiastes, which had a strong influence on Twentieth Century world
poetry. Here is the original Biblical text:

To everything there is a season.
And a time to every purpose under the heaven
A time to be born, and a time to die;
A time to plant, and a time to pluck that which is planted;
A time to kill, and a time to heal;
A time to break down, and a time to build up;
A time to weep, and a time to laugh;
A time to mourn, and a time to dance;
A time to cast away stones, and a time to gather stones together;
A time to embrace, and a time to refrain from embracing;
A time to get, and a time to lose;
A time to keep, and a time to cast away;
A time to rend, and a time to sew;

A time to keep silence, and a time to speak;
A time to love, and a time to hate;
A time of war, and a time of peace.

In the Bible, the narrator of the above verses speaks in a voice of authority to the community. The voice is declarative, aware that it speaks wisdom. Look what happened when Polish poet Tymoteusz Karpowicz borrowed this "list poem" format with its anaphorical repetition of the word "time," and transformed it into a post-World War Two landscape:

Ecclesiastes

there is a time of opening the eyes and closing the bed
[…]
time for the hair-brush and for the sparks in the hair
[…]
time for carrots peas and parsley
[…]
time for trussing chicken and releasing forbidden speeds for thought
time for cinema ticket or a ticket to nowhere
to a river perhaps perhaps a cloud
[…]
time from wall to wall   (87)

While Karpowicz announces from the start—the very title of the piece—his intent to correspond with the older text, the images, tone and use of detail do a great deal to transform the tone of the canonical litany. This onslaught of detail in Karpowicz's version—a cinema ticket, tomato soup, a hairbrush—offers its own metaphysics—homelier in comparison to the Ecclesiastical narrator's grand proclamations. Writing in post-war Europe, having witnessed the great acts of destruction and survival, Karpowicz's tone is both ironic and tender. His response is multilingual, multivocal, it refuses to console, and yet consoles. It allows the canonical form to enter into our world.

Another poet writing in the post–World War Two landscape, Paul Celan, offers us a very different take on what a "correspondence" with a canonical text may accomplish:

Corona

Autumn eats its leaf out of my hand: we are friends.
From the nuts we shell time and we teach it to walk:
then time returns to the shell. [...]

We stand by the window embracing, and people look up from
    the street:
it is time they knew!
It is time the stone made an effort to flower [...]   (29)

Celan's poem above is a very private, personal address. "It is time they knew!" Celan exclaims, as his repetition of "time" in the last five lines of the poem echoes the old text, giving it a chance to enter a Twentieth Century love lyric. If the speaker is addressing the public (as in Ecclesiastes), it is by standing with his lover by the window, embracing.

Yet another Twentieth Century poet who echoed this Biblical litany in a very personal way is Carlos Drummond De Andrade. In his poem "Your Shoulders Hold Up the World," he offers intense self-examination:

A time comes when you no longer can say:
    my God.
A time of total cleaning up.
A time when you no longer can say: my love.
Because love proved useless [...]

Who cares if old age comes, what is old age?
Your shoulders are holding up the world
and it's lighter than a child's hand [...]
Some (the delicate ones) judging the spectacle cruel

will prefer to die [...]
A time comes when life is an order.　　　(29)

The wisdom of Ecclesiastes is updated here to the Twentieth Century voice in a similar way as with the previous poems—the proclamatory public tone is replaced by the utterance of an individual, in this case, one persuading himself against suicide. This voice, although at times public, is not so interested in teaching others how to live—it is interested in voicing one human's need to survive. The struggle here is not so much with the community as it is with one's self. This, of course, reminds us of Yeats' great Twentieth Century statement that "argument with another is a rhetoric, argument with one's self is poetry."

Finally, Yehuda Amichai's poem "A Man in His Life" enters into confrontation with Ecclesiastes:

A Man in His Life

A man in his life has no time to have
Time for everything.
He has no room to have room
For every desire. Ecclesiastes was wrong to claim that.

A man has to hate and love all at once,
With the same eyes to cry and to laugh
With the same hands to throw stones
And to gather them,
Make love in war and war in love.

And hate and forgive and remember and forget
And order and confuse and eat and digest
What long history does
In so many years.

A man in his life has no time.

When he loses he seeks
When he finds he forgets
When he forgets he loves
When he loves he begins forgetting.

And his soul is knowing
And very professional,
Only his body remains an amateur
Always. It tries and fumbles.
He doesn't learn and gets confused,
Drunk and blind in his pleasures and pains.
In autumn, he will die like a fig,
Shriveled, sweet, full of himself.
The leaves dry out on the ground,
And the naked branches point
To the place where there is time for everything.   (158)

This ability to hate and love at once, in the same line, in the same moment, is perhaps one of the more characteristic attributes of many great poems from this era, whose "confusion" is not for the sake of mere linguistic fireworks, but to describe the joyfulness and terror of a human being in the Twentieth Century. Amichai, like the other poets before him, is able to go back to the origin of the Biblical text—but he does not merely update it for our own moment in time—he confronts it. His confrontation is personal: intimate just as much as it is public, the argument with the tradition becomes more powerful in its intimacy of address. The above group of Twentieth Century poets echoing the same origin could of course be much larger, and could make up an anthology in its own right. Such cases are not at all unusual. Thus, Faiz Akhmed Faiz of Pakistan was strongly influenced by the formal Persian tradition, and Garcia Lorca "corresponded" with traditions as various as *romanceros*, Arabic *qasidas* of medieval Spain, Gongora's metaphors, and the poetic expanse of Walt Whitman. Whitman, our American forebear, also deeply affected numerous Twentieth Century poets worldwide: Mayakovsky, Apollinaire, Pessoa, Neruda, Cesaire, Miłosz, Yona Wallach, and many others come to mind. Languages are many, says Voznesensky; poetry is one. If this is true, then perhaps an avid reader of poetry from around the globe may have a chance to glimpse into the heart of the art of poetry itself—of that which exists between languages.

Correspondence and Incantation

Your assignment today is to enter this "correspondence" — write a poem that adopts biblical form, rhythm, and incantation for your own means and needs. Feel free to use other poems as your examples.

Works Cited

Amichai, Yehuda (tr. Chana Bloch). *The Selected Poetry of Yehuda Amichai.* Berkeley and Los Angeles, CA: University of California Press, 1996.

Celan, Paul (tr. Michael Hamburger). *Poems of Paul Celan.* New York, NY: Persea Books, 2002.

Drummond de Andrade, Carlos (tr. Mark Strand). *Travelling in the Family.* Hopewell, NY: The Ecco Press, 1986.

Karpowicz , Tymoteusz. From *The Burning Forest,* Adam Czerniawski, Ed. Bloodaxe Books. North Umberland, UK: High Green, 1988.

ROBERT KINSLEY

COMMENTS ON THE ANAPHORIC POEM

I like this as a first poem exercise as it puts everyone on the same page—using the same repeated phrase—and gives all of us good starting points to engage poems.

The Anaphoric Poem

Write an anaphoric poem based on the strategy used by Greg Orr in his poem "A Litany." Your job is to use the repeated phrase "I remember" at least four times in the poem. The poem should be of average length—somewhere between fifteen and twenty lines and should focus on one event.

Here is an excerpt from the beginning of Greg Orr's poem:

I remember him falling beside me,
the dark stain already seeping across his parka hood.
I remember screaming and running the half mile to our house,
I remember hiding in my room.
I remember that it was hard to breathe
and that I kept the door shut in terror that someone would enter. . . . (4)

Work Cited

Orr, Greg. *City of Salt*. Pittsburgh, PA: University of Pittsburgh Press, 1995.

ROBERT KINSLEY

COMMENTS ON THE PHOTOGRAPH POEM

I like this exercise as it puts a physical object into play, it forces a writer to stay in one arena, and others in the class have a physical reference to the final poem.

The Photograph Poem

To write a photograph poem, you will need to find (and perhaps bring to a writing class or group) a photograph that has intense, serious meaning to you—of yourself, family, friends, or pets—but something that you would take with you if you could only take one photo out of a burning apartment. In class, start by free-writing while looking at and thinking about the photograph. After doing this for twenty minutes or more, exchange photos with someone: that person, who has no connection to the photo, free-writes on what it is that he or she thinks haunts one in the photograph.

The assignment then is to write a poem based on your own photograph: it has to be clear to a reader, either by the title or a reference in the poem, that this is based on a photograph, and the poem needs to stay within the photograph. This is not as easy as it first appears.

HERB KITSON

COMMENTS ON RE-WRITING HISTORY

Students often have trouble coming up with creative topics to write about. A good ice-breaker, though, is writing about history or current events, where students re-tell an occurrence from their own perspective. This gets the students outside of themselves. Poetry of a social nature is easy because students do not have to invest too much of themselves in the exercise. They can be anonymous and let their creativity flow from a negative-capability approach.

Re-Writing History

Spend a few days reading your local paper or listening to the news. Select an event that appeals to you—one that you think is noteworthy or one that you can relate to. Do you really think that this event is straightforward? Is the article or news program being truthful? What do you think is going on behind the scenes? Can you re-tell this event in such a way as to make it seem more like what you think really happened? Be creative. Use your imagination. Be fanciful if you wish and re-write history according to your liking. You are the reporter or newscaster and are presenting the material for the first time. Use this assignment to be preposterous if you want. Make the event that you are writing about your own.

PHYLLIS KOESTENBAUM

COMMENTS ON A PROSE POEM IN FIVE DAYS

Unlike the sonnet and the villanelle, the prose poem cannot be taught but, through practice, you can learn to "write" your life, your particular life, private and public. The prose poem is the vehicle for transcribing your life: the inner life, subversive thoughts and all; the world outside your writing room; and the people you live with and meet, from the closest relationships to daily trivial encounters with supermarket clerks and the UPS carrier. Your life is not imposed on the poem. The poem does not contain your life. Your life *is* the poem. And what makes the poem, which is your life, distinct is the vocabulary with which, all day long and in your dreams, you speak to yourself—its rhythm, inflection, syntax, diction. The unlined, margin-to-margin sentences of the prose poem are, I believe, absolutely the right form for the large swaths of experience and feeling that inform these conversations.

The only difference between a prose poem and a lyric or a narrative poem is the line, which the prose poem, because it's prose, doesn't have. However, the prose poem uses all the devices of poems—image, metaphor, repetition, internal rhyme—and without the support of the line sometimes uses them—especially repetition—more intensively.

One thing the prose poem is not is poetic prose. A story or a novel can be poetic prose but a prose poem should not be. The poetry in the prose poem comes from the poet's thoughts. And though there is real poetry in that verbalizing and there are beautiful prose poems, the prose poem I am suggesting you practice writing does not aim for beauty. The beauty in the prose poem comes from the music of the thinking, more atonal than melodic, more Alban Berg than Mozart. Indeed, the prose poem may seem flat, for irony is a tool the prose poet likes to use. She (or he) regards life with a cool eye—all of life, the ugly too. Often the prose poem is downright funny, but not laughing out loud funny. The prose poet is not a standup comic.

It helps to be writing regularly in a notebook, to get used to how you speak to yourself about the objects, events and experiences that fill your days, to get used to how your sentences move from one to the next. Write in a notebook for ten minutes (timed minutes) at least five days of the week. Understand, you are not writing in your notebook to get material for your prose poem, though what you write there will reveal the contents and modus operandi of your conscious and unconscious mind. There you get rid of the detritus of petty annoyance, conflict; record your dreams; express your feelings. The prose poem may also embody emotions, for it is after all a poem, but you will not express them in the same way as in your notebook, rather focus on the life itself, not how you feel about the life. Reproducing that life exactly will convey the emotional timbre of that life, the life only you have.

You may find it helpful to have a subject in mind for your prose poem. The subject could be big or small, as big as a childhood humiliation, as small as giving instructions for an activity (see Julio Cortázar's "Instructions on How To Cry"), or you could describe the stapler or the paperweight on your desk, or the last year of high school, a failing friendship, your body. Or you could write about your mother, say the clothes she wore—anything about your mother is excellent material for a prose poem. But you don't have to have a subject. You can just sit down and write, a kind of free-write, except that you expect what you are writing to become a prose poem.

A Prose Poem in Five Days

(If possible five consecutive days, if possible at the same time each day—I like to start on Monday, finish on Friday)

Day One: Free-write from nowhere (if you have a subject free-write from that). Just start writing. Start from the first word. Write what happened yesterday or making oatmeal today—write about your shoes—war—sex—anything. Don't think; just write. The main thing is not to think it is a poem, especially not a good poem, for then you will needle yourself to write beautiful language, not the gritty prose that comes from your everyday life.

Your prose should be blunt, tactile, honest—uncomposed. You are not to compose this writing; you are just to write it. It is not a poem—yet. There may be few images or no images. Nature may not even enter: on Day One, no trees, grass or sky.

Hopefully you're writing at a white heat, racing the clock. Time this writing as you did your notebook writing. Give yourself from ten to twenty minutes (the prose poem I'm suggesting ought not to go beyond one and one-half pages) and decide that time before you start writing. With that benign decision, you are setting the structure, a frame in which to fit the poem: *the prose poem is not formless.* And I suggest you write longhand, preferably with a favorite pen. Penciled writing looks unimportant. And no writing you do is unimportant. Don't read your timed writing. Put it away. This is essential. Feel triumphant: you have written a raw first draft of what will be a prose poem, have laid out the territory you will enlarge or amend, one or more pages of sentences to work on.

Day Two: Read what you've written—quickly. Cut without thinking (keep in the necessary; leave out the unnecessary). Mostly add. Follow your associations; the poem-to-be may get a little larger and more complex. Let it. Be sure your descriptions and the transcriptions of your thoughts are precise, to the point. Give it a title. You're getting the movement, the rhythm of the poem that is your life (the thread).

Day Three: Do deeper revisions—less putting in and taking out. Cut out transitions, leaving gaps, silence. Connections needn't follow a straight line. Syntax can link sentences subtly. Cut what's less interesting: you don't want to bore yourself. Be flashy, quirky, bizarre. Don't censor. Cut to tighten, to sharpen, to find areas that don't seem to belong together but actually do. Remove barriers of language that impede what you're beginning to sense is the *real* poem, the poem itself. This five-day prose poem ideally works better in one paragraph, though that isn't critical, as long as it's not longer than half your second printed page. Beyond that length, the prose overtakes the poetry and you run the risk of writing poetic prose, not a prose poem. A prose poem ought to be taken in as a short one-course meal, only one long thought with significant interruptions, everything relating to everything else, each sentence relating to every sentence, all of it held in the mind at one time, not wandering like a short-short or a regular story.

Of course, you can still add what comes to mind, sparingly, but still without inhibition—the poem is still in process. But you will undoubtedly want to add less as the structure you set on Day One increasingly firms, adheres, holds. By now the thread is apparent, bright or dark. And the rhythm of your thoughts—of your life—is beating on the page.

About the ending: endings are murder. End quietly, not with the burst of a lyric poem. The ending can arrive with a new insight, except don't have it summarize or conclude like an essay or the resolution of a short story.

Day Four: Breathe and breathe and read and read and do another edit, one that could require greater concentration for the prose poem is almost there. Again, don't be afraid to cut or add, though you probably won't want to do much of either.

Now type it or put it on the computer. Then read it once more from the printed copy and make the small cosmetic edits.

Day Five: Read; edit one more time. *You have completed your prose poem. Put it away.*

Next week, or many weeks or months later, go back to it and either leave it as is (this does happen) or fine-tune it. I've found that the fine-tuning is both easier and harder. Now I want my prose poem to be as good as it can be, sensational if possible. I want to be able to consider it as finished as I can make it, be content to leave it alone, to move beyond it, to move forward. You ought to feel satisfied if not jubilant. You may feel with these later revisions you have lost the inspired flow of the first days' drafts, but almost always the gain outdistances the loss. The prose poem is not merely a stream of associations in sentences.

POEMS RELATED TO PROSE POEM EXERCISE

Anne Carson: *Short Talks*: "On Waterproofing"; "On Sylvia Plath"
Julio Cortázar: "Instructions on How To Cry"
Lydia Davis: "Boring Friends"
Robert Hass: "A Story About the Body"
Helga M. Novak: "The Freezing Pan"; "The Rubber Gloves"

SAMPLE POEM

Birthday Girl

This happens a lot in restaurants. At the sushi bar, to my right, there are two men and a girl between them. The girl says she wants two scoops of ice cream: red bean and green tea. It's her birthday. The server says you can't order two scoops, only one scoop, so the girl says OK, then she'll have one scoop and one scoop. And indeed the server brings her one scoop in one dish and one scoop in another dish, two scoops, both of green tea because they're out of red bean. This is quite funny but not a joke. The birthday girl (and the chef calls her birthday girl—everything the chef says he says smiling) has amazing lips: how can I describe them. She could be an actress in a movie with those lips but I don't think she is an actress in a movie, with the two fellows, one on each side, ordering sushi as if it were free, until the two scoops in two dishes come, then only the two order and then the check comes, which my neighbor, hunched towards the lips girl, like my son sitting on his foot at my kitchen table and hunched towards me, puts down a single hundred for and the other fellow, hunched like the other fellow towards the girl with lips, for his half tosses a card. Some years ago I wrote a poem about people in a movie theatre in San Francisco's Japantown eating noodles from styrofoam cups, a poem I never completed: no matter what form I put it in I couldn't complete it. To my left there is a young woman with the smallest wrists imaginable. A man old enough to be the chef's father, carrying a wooden boat, sits down at the other end of the emptying bar. The chef almost stops smiling, almost beads with sweat (from time to time, between sushi preparations, he wipes his face with the side of a hand, then wipes the hand on his white chef trousers). The boat man wears glasses. I've never seen a sushi chef with glasses but why shouldn't a sushi chef like a surgeon wear glasses. How respectfully, though rapidly, the chef slices the fish he's slicing, almost as if he's slicing himself. "Thank you," "Thank you," he and I say as I leave, one *Thank you* each. In the poem I didn't complete, my movie neighbor and his, who knew each other outside the movie, said: "How **are** you," "How **are** you," one *How are you* each.

—Phyllis Koestenbaum

MARJORIE MADDOX

COMMENTS ON EATING POETRY, CLEANING CHEMISTRY, SURFING ALGEBRA

In an effort to 1) encourage experimentation with the surreal and/or 2) make literal a cliché, try the following exercise.

Eating Poetry, Cleaning Chemistry, Surfing Algebra

Discuss the following poem by Mark Strand:

Eating Poetry

Ink runs from the corners of my mouth.
There is no happiness like mine.
I have been eating poetry.

The librarian does not believe what she sees.
Her eyes are sad
and she walks with her hands in her dress.

The poems are gone.
The light is dim.
The dogs are on the basement stairs and coming up.

Their eyeballs roll,
their blond legs burn like brush.
The poor librarian begins to stamp her feet and weep.

She does not understand.
When I get on my knees and lick her hand,
she screams.

I am a new man,
I snarl at her and bark,
I romp with joy in the bookish dark.

After discussing the above, come up with a list of eight nouns/subjects. Write these on the board. A typical list may look like this:

Poetry
History
Algebra
Music Appreciation
Biology
Psychology
Nineteenth Century Literature
Chemistry

Next, generate a list of eight verbs. Put these on the board in a second column.

Poetry	Singing
History	Snoring
Algebra	Scrubbing
Music Appreciation	Surfing
Biology	Dancing
Psychology	Hyperventilating
Nineteenth Century Literature	Whispering
Chemistry	Screaming

Choose one word from each column for the title of your own poem draft, for example, "Surfing History." Your individual task for the next fifteen to twenty minutes is to "literalize" your title in your poem, using Mark Strand's poem/work as a model.

Finally, as a group, discuss poetry and the process of discovery by examining the poems just drafted.

MARJORIE MADDOX

COMMENTS ON THIS IS THE COLOR

This exercise forces students to focus on detail and tone by describing something ordinary (in this case color) in a more specific and unusual way.

This Is the Color

Needed: The poem "This Is the Color" or another poem that defines a color.

We are going to describe something that we take for granted—color—in a way that conveys emotion, insight, and situation. First, we'll list six colors on the board. What do you see "lurking" in each of the words; that is, what moods or emotions are sometimes associated with these particular colors? What situations? Let's put this second list next to the first one.

Next, we'll work on combining the two lists to draft a poem. Let's begin with what you associate with each color. What general connotations does each color have? Personal connotations?

Now, write down a color on a piece of paper and pass this around the circle until your teacher tells you to stop. Once you've received "your" color, you'll begin drafting a poem using the working title "This Is the Color." (Later, feel free to change the title; for now, though, this will help get you started.) Write for at least twenty minutes. Here's my version of this poem to give you some ideas:

This Is the Color

Blue and purple and black and all that bruises in a voice.
Here. Where the edge of words smeared across air
become sky. Where the slight swirl of cloud
divides not night from night, but layer from layer
as if a sound could be peeled into grays so thick
you could sift out teaspoons of light. No more.

This is the color I talk
summers when the heat sticks like a screen door,
prickles like a burn on the bottom of my foot.
This is your breath, left behind on a back porch,
your steps clicking.

Wrap me in the folds of a big black skirt,
quiet as cotton, as clothesline sheets
catching wind on an August night,
any sound but this: a man, crows in his eyes,
a woman, face eclipsed; now apart, now together,
hissing the day into dark.

—Marjorie Maddox

After a good twenty-minutes or so of writing, read your drafts out loud for
the group. Pause after each poem to discuss the following:

    What is lurking in this poem?
    How do you know this?
    What images make you believe this?

*For further discussion, these questions may be applied to the student
samples as well.

MARJORIE MADDOX

COMMENTS ON THIS IS YOUR LIFE: MAKING YOUR CHARACTER HIS/HER OWN PERSON

This is your life. Or is it? Too often in creative writing workshops, students strive to create characters completely like themselves. (Maybe you've heard a fellow student complain after a constructive peer suggestion, "But that really *is* how it happened!) Others haphazardly sketch a cardboard protagonist with little insight into how that person thinks, feels, acts, and reacts. To combat both, we'll use the following exercise to explore persona, voice, and poetic narrative.

This Is Your Life: Making Your Character His/Her Own Person

Prior to this exercise, my students are asked to turn in at least one long poem that retells a familiar story or myth from an atypical persona's perspective (i.e., the serpent in the Garden of Eden) or a long poem written in the voice of personae unlike themselves. In either case, I ask that they have enough writing so they are invested in their main character and *think* they know what the character is all about. This exercise is for a group that has done such an exercise recently. When you have done that, use the following instructions.

Today when you enter the class, do not talk. Instead, notice what I've written on the board, "This is your life. Please take a seat in the circle as your character." Thus, some of you may saunter to your seats; some may strut; some slouch or slink. All of these "character clues" will further prepare us for what follows. After you situate yourselves and adjust to your persona, I'll turn the lights off to focus us on the needed transformation. When I turn the lights back on, I will ask a long series of questions, and I'd like you to write down the answers—as your character—as honestly and thoroughly as you can.

Next, for a full ten minutes, I'll ask questions that range from the probing to the ridiculous. Focused solely on your characters, you are allowed only to write (not speak) your answers. Here are sample questions: What is your favorite thing to do on a Saturday night? What do you like to eat for breakfast? What is your greatest fear? What is your address? Do you believe in God? Why or why not? What is your most embarrassing moment? Who is your best friend? Your worst enemy? How do you take your coffee? Do you wear slippers? What is your least favorite time of the day? How do you feel about your mother? Why should we listen to you? Of what are you most ashamed? What is your worst habit? What are the full names of your siblings? How do you feel about each? How often do you brush your teeth? When was the last time you had sex? What do you least like about other people? Most like? What is your most painful memory? What is your deepest secret? How do you feel about the opposite sex? What do you most regret in your life? Were you named after anyone? If so, who? How do you feel about your father? What is your political affiliation? What is your favorite book? Where do you work? For how long? What color is your underwear? How often do you clean your kitchen floors? What is your worst nightmare? Do you add salt before tasting your meal? What is the most exciting thing you've ever done? Whom do you most admire? Why were you born? Such questions will force us as authors to know how and why our characters make the choices they do—how and why they react in situations both in and outside the scope of your poem.

Once you have several pages of notes "on yourselves," character by character, we will uncover more and more about each individual. Start by allowing each "character" to give a brief introduction of him/herself, usually four or five sentences that include such basic information as name, age, central conflict, time period, etc. Next, moving around the circle, each of you (also in character) will ask the spotlighted person at least two questions. Remember, these questions may be grand or simple, philosophical or practical. What follows should be a lively, thought-provoking, give-and-take that forces us to look between (and over and under) the lines of your developing narratives. "I didn't know this was my life," one of my previous students explained, "until I had to speak what wasn't even part of my poem." And speaking leads to writing that leads to a better understanding of the life which is taking shape before your classmates' eyes. Now, as the next step, write or rewrite the poem in your character's voice using this experience and all that you know about your persona.

GARY MARGOLIS

COMMENTS ON JAMES WRIGHT
WAS MY TEACHER

James Wright was my teacher, many years ago, one summer, in Buffalo, New York. He taught six students a course called, "Poets of Despair—Robinson, Frost, and Jeffers." We didn't know he would be diagnosed with lung cancer. We didn't know his transforming poem, "A Blessing," was set near the Mayo Clinic, where he would be a patient near his friend Robert Bly's home.

James Wright Was My Teacher

Wright begins "A Blessing," "Just off the highway to Rochester, Minnesota,/ Twilight bounds softly forth on the grass." And moves to the expressive— "There is no loneliness like theirs"—referring to two Indian ponies, and ultimately to the poem's own realization, "Suddenly I realize/That if I stepped out of my body I would break/into blossom."

How could I possibly create the opportunity for my college and New England Young Writers' Conference high school students to encounter, in their writing, these types of straightforward and lyrical lines, an epiphany of their own? To have the experience of finding and being found by a line of poetry. I have used two strategies to engage this possibility.

1. The first assignment, then, is to pick a place most familiar to you and begin a poem, "Just off the highway to…" and then write with as much detail and range of language as possible that includes words like "Rochester" and "bounds softly forth."

2. In a similar vein of engaging the first few lines of a poem, the second assignment is to start a poem as if writing a letter, beginning "Dear…." James Wright teaches us to hear the wings in a poem, to let a poem begin anywhere it needs to.

SEBASTIAN MATTHEWS

COMMENTS ON MIXED UP CONFUSION:
A PROSE POEM EXERCISE

For this exercise, bring books of photos about things like jazz, daily living, urban renewal. Frank's *Americans*, Arbus, or any *Life* anthology will do. *Let Us Now Praise Famous Women*. Weston's *Nudes*. Etc.

Mixed Up Confusion: A Prose Poem Exercise

Gather together a dozen books of photography. Go for the ones full of people—with lots of faces and bodies in space. Make sure to include a few landscape collections, Ansel Adams or The Sierra Club.

Now arrange the books into four groups of three or three groups of four. (Depending on the odd-even thing, the instructor may have to join in.) Have the students settle into groups—one group per table—placing a book in front of each participant. Let them flip through their book, eventually settling on a single image. This should take a minute or so, nothing too deep. Whatever looks interesting.

Now you're ready to go. Here are the instructions for the exercise. You can read them as is or ad lib.

+ Write what you see in front of you, sketching with words. No extra emotion, no narrative take, as little psychological insight as possible. Capture what's inside the frame of the image. Ask yourself: *What do I see? What's going on inside the box?*
+ After five minutes, pass the books to your left and do the same thing with your neighbor's image. Just draw a line under the first paragraph of prose and start again. Same principles apply. Remember, sketch with words what you see in front of you.
+ Do this one more time. You will now have three photo sketches, one after the other.

- Give your paragraphs to someone in your group. They should now read slowly, circling three or four phrases or passages in each paragraph. Pick out the little runs of language that create sharp visuals. Circle any bright or musical phrase. No need for the circled phrases to relate to one another. This should also take about five minutes.

- Now hand the page over to someone who hasn't seen it before. (Don't worry; it sorts itself out.) Take the circled phrases and copy them down on a new page so that a list of lines is created (making sure to give each phrase or passage its own line). After reading through these lines a few times—possibly reordering them—write a brief title at the top. As a last thought, assign the lines a mood state, such as "strung out and nervous" or "one too many mornings and a thousand miles away" or "drunken delusion" or "snowy morning horniness." Again, no more than five minutes.

- Give the lines back to their author. The original paragraphs are tossed in the trash, so the poet should be faced only with the raw material for a prose poem. The lines before them are their lines but *out of context.*

- Now it's time to write a prose poem (quick definition: a paragraph of prose that carries the rhythms and music of poetry in its lines). You can use any of the photos opened on the table or ignore them. You should feel free to tweak the phrases, fit the passages where needed, add new material, etc. You can allow the title to guide you and choose to take up the challenge of the tossed off "mood," which might help you hone in on the tone. Or throw them both out and concentrate solely on the lines.

(Hint: try writing this to someone else, real or imagined, maybe even someone in the photo.)

- Stop after 20-30 minutes and read the poems aloud in a circle. Let people respond to what they notice going on in each poem. Try to avoid suggesting ways to revise, if at all, until the very end of each discussion.

Ask the class what they liked about the exercise (what did it show them?) and what they hated about it. The idea here is to give up authorship for a while, and to provide the editing mind a hunk of raw prose. *What shines? What sparkles?* And then to have your words handed back to you. *What's your obsession? What are you writing about?* To watch yourself turn the material at hand into something new. To trust your voice and to downplay narrative continuity.

REBECCA MCCLANAHAN

COMMENTS ON ONE AT A TIME ALL AT ONCE: NOW COLLIDING WITH THEN

Poems based on actual life experiences often fail to achieve a life of their own, to rise above a mere re-telling of events. One way to allow imagination to work its way into memory is through a collision of past and present events. Gary Miranda uses this technique in "Horse Chestnut," a startling poem in which a present event—the speaker of the poem viewing a horse chestnut tree through a window—collides with several past events. The chronology of the poem doesn't reflect a calendar progression. Rather, it reflects the flow of the speaker's mind. The events, though they occurred months or years apart, occur simultaneously within the telling: a boy falls from a tree; a girl named Judy Cole puts five chestnuts into her mouth; a mother scolds the boy for climbing the tree; a young woman named Judy Cole is named Miss Seattle; a doctor administers Novocain; the boy marries; the boy gets sixteen stitches.

In Miranda's poem, there is little connective tissue tying the events together. Instead, the events are pushed up against each other with little or no stated transitions between them. The collision among the events, rather than the events themselves, shapes the poem, and what emerges is a new text altogether, a reconstructed view of how the mind makes sense of random memories.

One At a Time All At Once: *Now* Colliding With *Then*

If you wish to explore the relationship among memories rather than merely record the events themselves, try this exercise. First, choose two or more memories that seem related in some way—by theme, emotion, character, place, or recurring image. You can write one long draft, moving freely from one memory to another as organic connections reveal themselves. Or you can write about each memory separately, then later combine the pieces to reveal organic connections. You might use scissors and tape, physically cutting each memory into small pieces—lines, words, phrases—then reassembling the pieces so that the past and present events collide with each other in new ways. Don't use transitions or connective tissue to try to tie the pieces together. Instead, allow the juxtapositions, the leaps in time and space. The result may feel disjointed at first, but if you work with the pieces as if they were pieces of a jigsaw puzzle, you may find they connect in interesting ways.

SCOTT MINAR

COMMENTS ON STRETCHERS

In his infamous introduction to Mark Twain's novel, Huck Finn tells us that Twain stretches the truth of his story sometimes. These "stretchers" as Huck humorously calls them, are duly noted and implicitly sanctioned by the main character because Twain, as Huck puts it, "mostly . . . tells the truth." The goal here will be to play with ideas of truth and lies. Everyone knows poems are supposed to use or reveal truths, but what if they use lies instead? This inversion may create new "weather" or unusual thinking, which can sometimes be a door into things that can escape conscious searching.

Stretchers

Write a draft of a poem based on lies, but like a good artist/liar distort both the truth and the lies to some effect that seems revealing or illuminating to you. For example, you might title your poem "Vicious Lies," then say nice things about everyone you know. Or you might title your poem "Secrets and Lies," then fill it with the most obvious truths you can think of. Clichéd phrases using the words "lie" or "lies" may be good frames for this exercise, but there will also be many variations on how to enter a poem draft like this. Try to find the truth inside the lie or the lie inside the truth. Play with your own (and our) understanding of the "boxes" that "truth" and "lie" are, and try to open them up. When you find that you want to settle on truths or lies in your poem draft, pull the rug out and change the terrain.

SCOTT MINAR

COMMENTS ON THE IMAGE MIRROR

Our emotional lives are complex. But tapping them can be instructive and interesting sometimes. This exercise gives us practice at one of poetry writing's primary skills: expressing emotion through imagery without using clichés.

The Image Mirror

Take out a sheet of paper and write down exactly how you feel, the many ways you may feel right now. Just write freely and explore your feelings. Start with "Today, I feel. . ." and fill in the blank space with an emotion and some detail. Start this sentence five times and try to come up with five different answers. Compose a poem only of these statements, no imagery: no pictures, stories or sensory perceptions at all.

Next, take out a second sheet of paper. Look over the draft you have written—then write a second poem doing exactly the opposite. Compose this poem of only images or "word pictures" that communicate the same things your first poem does. In your second poem you may not use emotion words: sad, angry, happy, etc. Let the images, narrative (descriptions can move), or pictures do the work for you.

SCOTT MINAR

COMMENTS ON THE INEFFABLE POEM

It's important to remember when we are writing poems that we are making art more than we should be "filling a mold." As a great golfer once put it, "Don't forget to let the mystery into your shots."

The Ineffable Poem

My friend, Swedish poet Ingela Strandberg, has an inimitable style because her poems are ineffable, though not entirely. This is a deliberate strategy using suggestion and implication to get "between the lines" and inside of things that are too hard to talk about—because the words, frankly, have run out and understanding or resolution are not possible. People who feel despair sometimes reach such a mental and emotional state. Ingela's translator Göran Mamlqvist notes that her memories are "unavailable to the reader," for example: a frequent feature of such poetic strategies. Here is the beginning to one of her poems (it goes on for another four pages):

> I stand at the gas station.
> Everything is open around me in me.
>
> I am getting old time
> blows straight into me through me.
>
> I don't know how I shall face. It.

Clearly, the poet isn't concerned with punctuation or other anchors to reality and/or convention. Yet, the poem is not entirely off the wall. We can see it channeling very strong emotions, perhaps even uncontainable ones, quite efficiently through either descriptive mysticism or metaphor (Is there a difference?): "time / blows straight [...] through me." It is, of course, absurd to say or to write something like this, and that is precisely what makes it so beautiful. Ingela's poems often have more in common with an Ingmar Bergman film than they do with what we call poetics or poetic strategies.

In order to approach the Ineffable Poem, try this. Imagine that the details of your life don't matter, yet all of the powerful emotions in it do. Imagine further that you or your avatars are characters in a conceptual film: a grainy, black-and-white in a real place filled with silence and portent, perhaps wind; and infused as well with an atmosphere of big ideas and mythic, collective human feelings or experiences. These are your true feelings, your authentic emotions. Now simply describe this scene, but as you do so take a few liberties—just a few—with the language, punctuation or phrasing in order to make what you are doing both stark and original.

PS You'll know this is working if you see a spirit-muse peeking from behind what you write, if it gives you a chill or makes it hard for you to focus on what is being said because it is all so compellingly strange.

SCOTT MONCRIEFF

COMMENTS ON CARMEN MIRANDA

Sometimes it's nice to come to class with a surprise, as I did on the day we did an unannounced project.

Carmen Miranda

For my class, I told the students we would all have an hour to write a 100-word poem on Carmen Miranda. None of us knew anything about her (I had heard of her), but I mentioned that there was some video of her on YouTube and a Wikipedia entry. I dismissed everyone to check the source material and write, with instructions to return in an hour with the finished poem.

All writers know that it's sometimes stimulating to work with very short deadlines. You may not get your best work, but you might get something you can work with later. Also, this relieves us from the debilitating pressure to have to be good all the time, which can lead to safe mediocrity. Under time pressure we may throw caution to the wind and go in a direction we wouldn't have imagined.

Here are the constituent parts of the Carmen Miranda experiment, which of course may be used with Carmen Miranda or some other person of interest:

- One-hour time limit
- Everyone starts with a level playing field
- Common source material
- Gather together at end of the hour to share results—often great fun

Variations:

- The common words poem (where everyone has five or six common words to fit into, say, a ten-line poem written in half an hour)

- The common line poem (everyone has to fit one reference line into their poem)
- The common title poem

SCOTT MONCRIEFF

COMMENTS ON THE VILLANELLE

When I teach formal poetry, I tend to emphasize "easier" forms like the limerick, the ballad, working up to the sonnet. Because of their length and complex repetitive forms, the villanelle and the sestina are extremely challenging for any poet, much less an undergraduate. Nevertheless, sometimes a student will rise to the occasion and amaze herself and her classmates. Offer the villanelle as an option in a formal poetry section. It will demonstrate, perhaps even more than the sonnet, how creativity can flourish within and because of constraints.

The Villanelle

In order to try your hand at one, here are the constituent parts of a villanelle:

- typically uses pentameter lines
- six stanzas: five tercets and a quatrain
- only two rhymes: aba aba aba aba aba abaa
- line one repeats as lines 6, 12, and 18
- line 3 repeats as lines 9, 15, and 19

Tip: Poets will cheat a little bit by making small variations in the words and punctuation of their repeated lines; actually, this is one of the features that adds interest and creativity to the form.

* For well known examples, see Dylan Thomas's "Do Not Go Gentle" and Elizabeth Bishop's "One Art": these are classics. But the form has also found many contemporary users.

SAMPLE POEM

Cruise

Superabundant fun, joy squared, Pauline
decided as she passed her menu back:
"Pacific Salmon with Dill Mousseline."

Seven days to live a libertine—
massages, facials, rock 'till dawn, blackjack:
Superabundant fun, joy squared. Pauline

tried sunsets, romance, shows and magazines
and bargaining for tourist bric-a-brac.
Pacific Salmon with Dill Mousseline

was not so good the second time. The sheen
of sexy salt spray skin began to crack.
Superabundant-fun-impaired, Pauline

began to think herself, joy-squared-unkeen.
That night the waiter asked; her face turned black.
"Pacific Salmon with Dill Mousseline?"

And while her lip hung on a nectarine,
her mind kept clacketing down one dismal track:
Pacific Salmon with Dill Mousseline,
superabundant fun, joy squared, pall e'en.

—Scott Moncrieff

SHARONA MUIR

COMMENTS ON THEME AND COINCIDENCE

What is a theme? It comes from the Greek *thema*, a "thing put in place," or a logical proposition—a way of introducing order by marking out one thing as significant so that other things can relate to it. We all know what a theme is in music or literature—it's that recognizable piece that keeps coming back, with various changes, while the rest of the composition also changes in relation to it. *

But what is a theme in *your* poetry? Think of it as the equivalent of rhyme in a different mode: theme is the ordered development of coincidence. Or, you could think of it as a sort of serious pun made with subject matter.

In Li-Young Lee's book *The City in Which I Love You*, for example, there is a theme of consumption, eating and being eaten in the natural cycle: you can see it in food imagery quite a bit, and in other ways too. You can think about it in one poem (e.g., the roast duck and fish in "The Cleaving") or across his work. We can speak of themes in a particular poem, or across a larger body of work. And, of course, a poem can have several themes.

* Craft Concepts Related to Themes: When you deliberately put themes in your poem, you are working with craft concepts that are both narrative and figurative. Your theme will be part of the poem's *plot*, but will also likely function as a *metaphor*. After writing your poem, check your Editorial Toolkit* to see how your theme is working on its narrative and figurative levels.

Theme and Coincidence

Search your memory and find a day, or a time period, when you noticed coincidences. Write them down. These are your "things put in place." Was there a reason why you noticed them? Would you have noticed them under other conditions? If your friend hadn't given you a book about caterpillars, would you have noticed the caterpillar on the dangling leaf? And the caterpillar tractor on the road afterwards? How did they make you feel, and what did you think about? What did the coincidences reveal to you about your thoughts and feelings?

Write a poem in which your coincidences are the themes.

SAMPLE POEM

In this poem, I have used the *theme* of elements: fire and water. The *coincidence* that I observed was the way that a fire, having burned for a long time, comes to resemble water in two ways—in its rain-like sound, and its blue color. This coincidence suggested the poem's *plot* in which an old fire tries to imitate water—and the poem's *metaphor* of fire and water as two different kinds of personalities or lives. The metaphor suggests that while time limits what we may become, we gain self-knowledge and wisdom (like seers) from grasping the choices that have made us who we are.

An Old Fire

has sunken on her wide bed
of red-hot coals. Air curls over them
and they ripple, like pebbles underwater,
making a ticking sound
like light rain coming down.

Old fire imitates her opposite, water,
the element she never was.
All she can become, at this late date,
is a blue skein, a blue knowing
out of nowhere

if not out of error and fate,
that shrinks to a blue seed
on the red lip of charcoal. Witch-seer,
smoke-thread.

—Sharona Muir

* Editorial Toolkit

Prosody

___ Cadence: Recited aloud, does it sound good? Are stressed and unstressed syllables where you want them? Is there variety as well as consistency?

___ Meter: If this is a poem in a metric form, is it regular and natural?

___ Mimesis: Does the poem's sound match and/or enhance its meaning? Think: cadence, alliteration, assonance, onomatopoeia.

___ End-stopped lines: Are they creating lag? Should they be enjambed?

___ Run-on lines: Do they go on too long? Are the line breaks interesting? Do they lead the reader to the next line?

___ Rhyme: Is it natural and compelling? Is there internal rhyme as well, and does it enhance the poem?

Composition

___ Title: Does it spark interest and add meaning? Do you want it to supply context?

___ Lines: Is each line as active and as interesting a unit as it can be? If there are less active lines, do they contribute to the poem's pacing and readability?

___ Stanzas: Can you identify each stanza's purpose in the poem's overall composition? Do the stanza breaks fall where you want them to? Do they aid, or detract from, continuity, context, and atmosphere?

___ First and Last: Are the first and last lines memorable and effective? Do you want to find a different rhetorical strategy for opening or closing?

Metaphor and the Senses

___ Controlling metaphor(s): Is it (are they) clear and focused?

___ Metaphors generally: Are the metaphors clear and resonant? Does the poem avoid closed metaphors and mixed metaphors?

___ Concrete details: Are the concrete details fresh, specific and true? Are there enough of them? Do they conjure up a scene, mood or subject to the reader's imagination?

___ Sensory details: Do the sensory details surprise and delight you? Do they smack of the real thing? Do they intensify or change your experience of the real thing? Do they work with the controlling metaphor, or distract from it?

___ Abstractions: Is the abstract language grounded in concrete details, images, and connotations? Or if you want to avoid concretization, is the abstract thought compelling and original enough—does it have a poetic presence?

Plot and Narrative

___ Context: Does the poem assume knowledge that the reader does not or may not have? Should you clarify, or elaborate? Can you provide clues to the reader at appropriate points?

___ Continuity: Does the poem jump around in time and space, or from topic to topic? If so, is the logic of the transitions clear? Can you make it clearer? Should you omit some jumps? If you want to mystify your reader, is there enough connection for the reader to enjoy the guessing game?

__ Point of View: Do we know who is speaking the poem? Is the point of view consistent and believable? If there are characters in the poem, are they adequately evoked? (Cf. Amichai, "Poets are lazy novelists.")

__ Settings: Are the settings of the poem adequately evoked, with concrete detail, vivid images, and/or metaphor? Think cinematically: what do you want your reader to see, hear, smell, feel, think?

__ Drama: Is the poem dramatic? Does it hold the reader's interest and create suspense with unresolved and unfolding questions or conflicts?

Sentences

__ Sentence completion: Are the sentences complete? If not, why not?

__ Sentence structure: Is the sentence structure clear and compelling? What about combining some sentences, using subordination, to make the poem move faster or to integrate separate bits of information? Do you want to break any long sentences? Do you want more variety in the sentence structure? Can you remove unnecessary words and phrases?

__ Syntax: Is the syntax interesting and effective? Does it help to pace and control the reader's perceptions?

__ *Verbs! Say it with verbs!:* Volcanoes, for instance, "open their coral lips/ and cities—ooze —away." Are the muscles of English, the verbs, carrying the poem's weight?

__ Diction: Is the diction natural and appropriate to your tone and subject? A poem doesn't have to sound like the way you talk—but avoid saying things in a poem that you could never say naturally.

* Editorial List

Here are nine basic elements to think about while working on a poem. (Consult the Toolkit for greater detail.) Use this sheet to comment on your poem's progress, and to ask questions about it. *Attach a copy of this completed worksheet to each copy of the poem that you're bringing to workshop.*

1. What's the poem about—which particular/universal human experience?

2. What are its controlling metaphors (any mixed metaphors?)

3. What about context? (setting, background, information)

4. What about continuity? (transitions, chronology, logic, framing devices)

5. What about the senses? (concrete details and images, atmospheres?)

6. Is there an effective cadence and/or metrical scheme?

7. What about rhyme? (internal, external, slant, true, rhyme schemes?)

8. What do the first and last lines try to achieve?

9. What about sentence issues? (structural variety, syntax, verbs, diction?)

DZVINIA ORLOWSKY

COMMENTS ON RAGING FIRES, WARM EMBERS

Read the following passage:

The Enchanted Desna
By Alexander Dovzhenko (Ukrainian film-maker, literary stylist 1894-1956)
—translated from Ukrainian by Dzvinia Orlowsky

Pleasant & Unpleasant (excerpt)

Trembling, tucked into myself, I recalled the Last Judgment. I looked up at the swallows and sighed. How helpless I was lying in Grandfather's boat and how schooled of unpleasant and bad things. How unpleasant it is when Grandmother curses at me or when long rain pelts down and doesn't want to stop. How unpleasant when a leech clings to your leg, or when strange dogs bark at you, or a goose hisses around your feet, nips at your pants with a red beak. And how unpleasant to carry with one hand a large bucket of water or to weed or tear off side-shoots of tobacco. How unpleasant when Father comes home drunk and fights with Grandfather, then with Mother, then throws plates. How unpleasant to walk barefoot over wheat stubs or to giggle in church when something strikes you as funny. Riding in a hay-filled wagon about to tip over is unpleasant. It's unpleasant to look at a large fire, but pleasant to look at its embers. How pleasant it is to hug a foal. Or at daybreak to see your calf wandering in all by itself, to know it found its way home in the dark. How pleasant it is to wade in warm puddles after thunder or to catch a small pike with your bare hands, stir muddy water, or to watch someone slowly pull in a large net. How pleasant it is to find a bird's nest in the grass, to eat Easter buns and eggs. How pleasant when spring waters flood the house and everyone wanders all over, how pleasant to fall asleep in Grandfather's boat, in the fields of rye, millet, barley -- and in all grains while they were drying on the oven. And of course, the smell of drying grain is pleasant. It's pleasant to drag a sheaf to a stack, to walk around the stacks, grain spilled everywhere. It's pleasant when an apple thought sour turns out to be sweet. It's pleasant when Grandfather yawns, when bells ring out on a summer evening. It's also pleasant—and this I loved most—when Grandfather talked with a horse or foal as if they were human. I loved when out of the darkness on the road a voice called out "Peace to you!" and Grandfather replied: "And may God grant you peace!" I loved when a big fish tossed in the lake or in the purple stillness of the Desna at sunset. I loved to lie in a wagon, returning home from the meadow, to look up at the star-filled sky. I loved to drift off to sleep—when the wagon pulled around to the house and I was carried, asleep, inside. I loved the sound of wheels screeching under wagons heavy with harvest in August. Birds chirping in the garden and in the field. I loved swallows in barns, rails in meadows. I loved the splash of spring water. At twilight, the cry-croak of frogs during a rainfall in a bog. I loved the songs of girls—carols, songs of the New Year, the coming of spring, the harvest songs. I loved the thud of apples in the orchard at dusk when they fall unexpectedly into the grass. A certain mystery and sadness, the inevitability and law that out of what seemingly ends, come the pleasant things of this world. I loved thunder, although it scared Mother, the downpour and loud wind for the gifts they brought to the orchard.

•

When the young speaker, Sashko, hides in fear from his cursing great grandmother for stealing carrots from her garden, he leads the reader through a profoundly beautiful meditation in which he contemplates all the pleasant and unpleasant things he has, at a tender age, already been schooled in. He notices life's curious contradictions: the abundantly filled hay wagon that, too full, tips along the river bend and finds itself empty, the fallen apple thought sour that turns out to be sweet (see excerpt).

Based on my translation from Ukrainian of Alexander Dovzhenko's novella, *The Enchanted Desna,* this exercise invites students to explore the "unpleasant" and "pleasant" tapestries of their lives, as well as the precarious balance between both seemingly opposing worlds. It provides a critical step in helping students to understand dramatic dualities as they explore the images and textures of their personal knowledge. It is also particularly useful in redirecting beginning writers from their tendency to see life experiences as either all positive or all negative.

Raging Fires, Warm Embers: An Exercise in Dramatic Dualities

Read the Dovzhenko passage aloud and listen to the full musical cadence of syntax and the possibilities of language, the gathering effect of the speaker's voice as, prompted by the anaphora "it's pleasant; it's unpleasant," he negotiates the mixed blessings of emotional and natural landscape. Pay close attention to the order in which information is presented with regard to how it reinforces meaning and how it allows the emotional content/ voice of the poem to accumulate. Next, experiment with this type of syntax using long, complex sentences as well short ones. As you puzzle and reflect in words, you may utilize aspects of a list poem to jump-start thoughts. Second and third drafts should weave pleasant and unpleasant imagery to more accurately convey to readers the shape-shifting volatility of human emotion. You may choose to write this assignment in free verse, as an introduction to the prose poem form, or try your hand at both.

PEN PEARSON

COMMENTS ON WRITING THE
SONNET IN THREE STAGES

Writing a sonnet is like trying to solve a Rubik's cube. You twist and turn to make one side of the cube red, only to foil your hard work when you twist and turn to make another side green.

When we try to master the conventions of a sonnet, we often face similar challenges and frustrations. We write fourteen lines in iambic pentameter, but when we focus on the rhyme scheme, our efforts at rhyming muddy the poem's pattern of images or confuse its theme. Worse, we write a sonnet that sounds like it belongs in a cheesy greeting card, because its rhythm and rhymes are forced.

Writing the Sonnet in Three Stages: the Modern Sonnet, the Borrowed End-Rhyme Sonnet, and the Traditional Sonnet

A method of writing sonnets so that the form doesn't control the content—and so that we don't lose our minds in frustration—is in stages.

Stage One: The Modern Sonnet

In the first stage, you convey an idea, an emotion, or an anecdote in fourteen lines of ten syllables each, without worrying about iambic pentameter or end rhymes. The result will be a modern sonnet, a sonnet that adheres to the conventions of lineation and syllable count without adhering to the conventions of rhyme scheme and iambic pentameter. Moreover, its language will be natural, because you will have used the conversational rhythms of everyday speech. And the subject of the modern sonnet needn't be a love, though it certainly can be.

The anecdote for "After a Long Flight Luggageless, Amy Cried" came from a personal experience. A niece of a friend came to visit him, and her luggage was lost. The images of the crushable hat and sandals were supplied by the woman named in the title, my friend's niece. And, indeed, Masaba airlines provided the phrases "delayed" luggage, and "lost, lost," as well as the promise of the "$50 voucher." Because I had been writing modern sonnets when I heard about the incident, I decided to sketch the anecdote in a poem of fourteen lines of ten syllables each. (Note that some lines contain a few extra syllables.) Rather than find the exercise constraining, I found it liberating. Using the structure of a fixed form, however loosely conceived, helped me to contain the anecdote in a satisfying form.

I credit the first draft being nearly complete to four strategies. One, I "primed the pump" by listing images and phrases I wanted to include. I then ordered these images before writing any sentences. Two, that's right: I wrote sentences rather than lines. I then broke these sentences across lines, adding words or phrases, such as adjectives, to make each line ten syllables. (Note that only two lines end in a sentence boundary, indicated, in both these lines, by a question mark.) Three, the first draft had fifteen lines. I "cheated" by including the first line as the title in the final draft. Four, in the draft, the last phrase "with no hope" was the sentence "How could she?" (to play off the last phrase of the second line: "why shouldn't she"). But I wasn't happy with this sentence because it didn't conclude the poem with a satisfying "click." It took me only an afternoon to draft the poem, but four months to write the final phrase. If we're good students, writing poems teaches us patience.

After a Long Flight, Luggageless, Amy Cried

Without her crushable hat and new shoes
(sandals to survive the heat), why shouldn't she,
for how can anyone enjoy vacationing
(at her uncle's ranch in South Dakota)
sleeping in her husband's t-shirt, washing
her underwear each evening in the sink?
Surely Masaba Airlines would produce
her "delayed" luggage, though they couldn't say

where it had gone, only that if it were
"lost, lost," which they'd know in forty-eight hours,
she'd receive a $50 voucher—
good toward her next flight. But who wants to fly
without a crushable hat and new shoes
(sandals to survive the heat), with no hope?

—Pen Pearson

Stage Two: The Borrowed End-Rhyme Sonnet

In the second stage, you borrow the end rhymes of a sonnet you admire. (No, this isn't plagiarism. If you use a poem that's well known, such as "My mistress eyes are nothing like the sun" by Shakespeare, you create an allusion.) Write these fourteen end rhymes in the right-hand column of a sheet of paper or a word-processing document (sun, red, dun, head, white, etc.) Read through the end rhymes several times until a subject, an initial phrase, sentence, or line, or a series of images occurs to you. You may want to "prime the pump" by listing the phrases or images that you want your sonnet to include.

Now complete the lines of the poem, moving from top to bottom. If you get stuck, backtrack. Try modifying the last image or phrase until it provides a gateway to the next line or rhyme. At this point, don't worry about writing in iambic pentameter. Instead, write in your own voice. Also, don't view the borrowed rhyme scheme as a straightjacket. Feel free to modify end rhymes to suit the development of your subject. For instance, in "The Mt. Rushmore State," I changed "sun" in the first line to "sunset," and its complement in the third line "dun" to "don't." In addition, I changed the last word from "compare" to "rare," and I opted for "no" instead of "know."

Once you've completed a draft, reread it. If a line contains eight syllables, can you modify a noun or verb with a two-syllable adjective or adverb? For example, in the first line, I considered deleting "South" to make the line ten syllables. But I wasn't satisfied with either the new meaning or the rhythm, so I left it. Note that the underlying rhythm is iambic pentameter, but it's varied enough so that the rhythm is natural rather than plodding. Read your sonnet aloud and use your ear to iron out your sonnet's rhythms to your satisfaction, remembering to avoid a sing-song rhythm, unless that's what you're aiming for, perhaps for humorous effect.

The Mt. Rushmore State

What, I ask, is a South Dakota sunset
made of if not the same yellows and reds
Rothko and Dufy stole from God? And don't
other states envy our presidents' heads—
even Florida, which can boast of white
sand beaches? Washington's and Lincoln's cheeks,
though not as rosy, give as much delight
to tourists as the Pope's (and neither reeks
of perfume, unlike White House rose beds). No,
South Dakota's brilliant sunsets don't resound
like Niagara Falls; just the same, they go
well with the Black Hills, the Badlands, the ground
farmers till, and when they grace our skies, rare
is the native, even, who doesn't stop, stare.

—Pen Pearson

Stage Three: The Traditional Sonnet

Once you've mastered the first and second stages, you're ready for the third stage. In this stage, you create your own end rhymes, using the rhyme scheme of an English or an Italian sonnet, whichever you prefer. To make my task manageable, I chose to describe a photo of myself from my childhood in the traditional sonnet "Photo of a Cowgirl." Rather than just a strict description, however, I wanted to dramatize a story the photo suggested. To do so, I needed a conflict, whether explicit or implied; a climax; rising tension; and a resolution. And to do that, I needed to depart from the truth, the real story of my childhood, and use my imagination.

In the first quatrain, I described the cake in the photo. In the second quatrain, I described the birthday girl. I wanted the images in both quatrains to be "telling." In other words, I wanted them to be suggestive as well as appeal to the readers' senses. The phrase "angel food" contrasts with the birthday girl's expression of defiance. Her outfit questions whether or not she'll be happy in a man's world, suggesting a conflict between her dreams and their realization. In the third quatrain, the conflict escalates as the poem imaginatively flashforwards to the birthday girl's future. Last, the final couplet offers an unsettling resolution. Despite her wishes, the realization of her dreams is a dim hope.

Before writing, I "primed the pump" by jotting down images I wanted to include: piano bench, birthday cake, cowboy boots, a rearing horse, using the photo as a guide. I then ordered the images, knowing that I wanted to describe the scene spatially: first the cake, then a close-up of the candles and figure, and last the "little girl." I started with the image of the birthday cake on a piano bench. I knew "cake" would make a good end rhyme. When I first described the cake, I chose the phrase "chocolate mint" instead of "angel food." The fearless rider became "Clint" as I continued my description, while using end rhymes. I didn't like the direct reference to Clint Eastwood, however. And chocolate mint isn't the kind of cake kids like. Once I thought of angel food, I knew I could change "Clint" to "Dude." The rhymes of "girl/curl" and "hat/skirt" came easily because I had listed them when I "primed the pump." But if they hadn't, I would have fiddled with them, using the image of the little girl as a guide, just as I fiddled with the rhyme of "food/Dude." The third stanza came out of nowhere: lines dropped from the sky. I credit their dropping, however, to knowing that I wanted some sort of escalating tension. The idea of her having a son came first, the description of his fate followed. The last couplet was the hardest to write. Once again, however, I used the description I wanted to guide the phrasing. Because the sonnet began with burning candles, I knew they had to be blown out. The rhyme of "wishes/delicious" came in a second or third draft, but the phrase "will each candle wink shut" took months and many drafts to finally appear.

Photo of a Cowgirl

On a piano bench, her birthday cake—
seven-minute frosting and angel food;
on top, four burning candles and keepsake—
a rearing horse, his fearless rider, Dude.
To the left of Dude stands a little girl,
in cowboy boots, Western shirt and hat.
Her face is defiant, her lip a curl;
hands rest on the holster around her skirt.
In twenty years, she'll bear a restless son.
He'll roam their town: a cowboy on his range.
Instead of cattle, he'll rustle cocaine,
and die of an overdose: city mange.
Will each candle wink shut as she wishes
for horses? Will the cake taste delicious?

—Pen Pearson

JON PINEDA

COMMENTS ON BEACH COTTAGES: A REVISION FRAMEWORK

When Emily Dickinson wrote "I dwell in Possibility," she left a key under the mat.

Sometimes what poets build with words are moments that feel like rooms, where the reader might enter and *dwell* for a while. Some of these rooms might have doors, and these doors might open into other rooms, into other parts of a tenuous home. Or they might open onto the surface of the ocean. We don't know until we move further into this construction. Such is the limitless direction of "Possibility" to which Dickinson refers.

But generating drafts of poems is just the beginning. It gets us only to the framework. What that framework is, exactly, depends on the shifting states of influence, factors within the poet's writing process. Some drafts are image-driven, others by the sound of the words themselves. Some by combinations of those or other obsessions. The variations are numerous, but in each instance, it is usually a gathering together of impulses. It is here that mystery makes a home within the framework of drafts.

Certain words are chosen for whatever reasons, and these choices have the ability to build in momentum, through their relationship with other words, into a realized consciousness. In *Triggering Town*, Richard Hugo elaborates: "Assumptions lie behind the work of all writers. The writer is unaware of most of them." Revision allows the poet to view how implication fashions together such construction.

Consider Dickinson again: just as the verb *dwell* implies a home of sorts, there is, at the same instant, a hint of the obsessive—the act of dwelling *on* something (or in

Dickinson's case, dwelling *in*). This word choice allows the line to function on various levels simultaneously. I immediately think of Hamlet's declaration that he could be "bounded in nutshell and count [himself] a king of infinite space."

In the same way, poems can be rooms of infinite space.

In Dickinson's poem, the speaker describes the act of creation in relation to the eternal

("Paradise"). Despite this sense of freedom, though, there is also containment implied by the limitless potential that language affords. Such notions might hint at a kind of "writer's block"; that anything is possible is, on the one hand, empowering, and on the other, debilitating. But if we seek to engage with the language—constantly assessing and reassessing our relationship with the words chosen— then we willingly enter into the dwelling.

Beach Cottages: A Revision Framework

Here is an exercise for testing the framework of your draft:

1. If our houses were built on stilts, like beach cottages near the shoreline of a barrier island, the stilts would serve the purpose of not only keeping the houses level, in the way a brick foundation works, but the stilts would also function to keep the houses high, out of reach of flooding from storms— from whenever or wherever those storms may arise. Take a look at the basic construction of your poem. Have you used lots of nouns? Are the nouns in your draft dependent upon adjectives? Are prepositional phrases utilized to alter rhythms within the relaying of these noun/adjective images? Circle every noun in your poem and put a line through every adjective. Read your draft aloud without the adjectives. Is the impact of the image lessened by the absence of the adjective(s)?

2. Take all of the nouns out of your poem and write them on another page, in a list from the top of the page down. Are there more specific nouns you could use that would allow you to forgo the use of certain adjectives? Using this list, reverse the order of the nouns from the way they are currently presented. This is a quick way to review the materials in your poem. If you reinsert these nouns, in this new order, back into

the poem, how does that affect the draft's overall impact? Is your poem dependent upon a certain sequence of images? Does your poem build to some kind of epiphany? What happens if you reverse the order of the grouped images presented? How does that affect the construction of your draft? Remember Robert Frost's edict—"No surprise for the writer, no surprise for the reader."

3.   Using your initial draft again, draw a box around each verb. How are the verbs used in relation to the nouns? Do they put the nouns into motion, in an original way? Do the current constructions alter or affirm a reader's relationship to the image(s) evoked? Should they? Put a double line through every adverb. Read the poem aloud without the adverbs. Do your verbs need to be changed in order to exist without the use of these adverbs? List the verbs, in the same way you did with the nouns earlier, and reorder the sequencing of the verbs. Reinsert them into the draft. Are there any surprises from moments/images affected by the verbs that would, at first glance, be completely incongruent? Remain open to such surprises.

So much attention has been given to generating drafts, and for good reason—the poet must begin from somewhere; the reader must begin from somewhere—but as the framework for each draft goes up, various negotiations are set into motion: *Is this the right word here? Is the tone consistent? Does it need to be?* The questions will risk endless answers, but don't be discouraged.

     In revision, we should be able to create and, in turn, wreck what we must. We should be open to making the floor a window, the windows doors. As Dickinson expressed, "for an Everlasting Roof/ The Gambrels of the Sky—" our notions of the literal must be pliable. Our ability to embrace the inhospitable nature of revision must be constant.

ERIC POTTER

COMMENTS ON BIBLICAL
CHARACTER VOICE POEM

This exercise helps students create a voice other than their "own." It is meant to push them out of themselves and their own experience. Since many of my students have a Sunday school familiarity with the Bible, I assign a character from the Bible. The character and incident provided by the biblical passage give the students a loose framework within which they can create. (I often find that having some details given by the passage frees them to be more inventive.) I encourage students to look for ways to surprise readers by developing their characters "against the grain" of conventional ways of viewing that character.

Before the assignment, my students and I read and discuss a number of poems, paying special attention to how the poets create voice. After describing the voice in each poem, we focus on the ways it is a product of subject, angle of vision, diction (especially levels of formality), and sentences (length, type, use of subordination, fragments).

Biblical Character Voice Poem

Choose a biblical character from the list below (preferably one of the opposite sex) and write a poem in his or her voice. The poem should be related to this character's experiences as recounted in the Bible, but feel free to invent, using the biblical narrative as a jumping off point. You might consider the following questions:

1. What would this character talk about?
2. How might the character feel about what has happened?
3. What attitudes or emotions would the character display?
4. How would he or she sound?

You may write in any form you like (minimum 20 lines).

Dinah (Gen. 34)
Esau (Gen. 25-28 and 33)
Balaam's ass (Num. 22)
Jephthah's daughter (Judges 11:29-40)
Bathsheba (2 Sam. 11, 12)
Gadarene demoniac (Mt. 8:28-34)
Gentile woman whose daughter is healed (Mt. 15:21-28)
Lazarus (Jn. 11:1-44)
Woman who anoints Jesus' feet (Mk. 14:3-9)
Dorcas (Acts 9:36-43)
Philippian jailer (Acts 16:25-34)
Eutychus (Acts 20:6-12)

These are some passages that I have assigned over the years, though one could find plenty of other characters and incidents. Some passages get them focusing on less well-known characters, while others encourage them, I hope, to approach familiar territory with fresh eyes.

The biblical passages work especially well with my students and could work well with the majority of students elsewhere. The assignment could also work with other source material, such as secondary characters in well-known works of fiction or figures from fairytales or other popular stories.

LAWRENCE RAAB

COMMENTS ON MANY DEMANDS OR A DOG, A BEAR, OR A WOLF

Recently this has been the second assignment I give the students in my introductory poetry workshop. The first is much simpler and more expansive: write a poem based on a painting (or other work of art). The poem need not end up being about the picture, but has to begin with some image. Beginning, of course, is always the most difficult part of writing, and my aim here is to lure the students into responding to something visual rather than starting off with an idea. Look at pictures. Don't think about what you're going to do. Just write something down. When you can't come up with anything else to write, look at another picture. And so on. The aim is the accumulation of potentially interesting pieces of language, which could then go anywhere. And the additional aim is not to remain committed to whatever first gets written down.

This second assignment offers many seemingly unconnected tasks. Again I try to leap over the problem of beginning by offering eight lines from a first line index (Mark Strand's *The Contemporary American Poets*). The idea is to choose one and just start writing, and if that doesn't take you anywhere, choose another—a narrative variation on the pictures. This could be an assignment in itself, since it's useful to discuss three or four poems that all begin with the same line and see what opportunities the students seized or missed. In terms of missed chances, I've found that "You might come here Sunday on a whim" rarely leads to a convincing instructional poem, that "I dreamed that in a city dark as Paris" usually veers quickly away from the qualities of a dream or the presence of a dreamer, and that "I must explain why it is that at night, in my own house" almost never results in a poem that explains anything, or follows the urgency of those first three words, posits an attentive listener, or indeed any listener at all.

The four metaphors in the assignment are hard, and often seem stuck in later, like some kind of seasoning the student had overlooked from the original recipe. The length of the poem seems important, since I want the various demands to collide with each other. I don't want to give the students too much time—or too much space—to think. Thinking, of course, is always the problem. Smart academically well-prepared college students have been taught to plan ahead, to know their topics, to outline, and it's hard to convince them that all of this is useless—even hazardous—in beginning a poem. It's very difficult to get them to believe that they can trust what they don't know, what they aren't in control of.

Of course they don't know why a poem, finally, should include the name of a country, the first name of a person, a piece of clothing, one spoken remark in quotation marks, and a dog, a bear, or a wolf, and in fact there is no reason. I have no poem in mind that includes all of these elements. There's no trick here, no secret program, no ultimate solution. All these things need to be there just because I've said so. The students can—and do—complain. But my hope is for a useful tension between frustration and fun.

Some of these strictures turn out to affect the poem in very lively ways. The name of a country is easy to sneak in, but the person's first name tends to suggest an actual human being, rather than the vaguely symbolic personages that beginning poets are attracted to. Even more striking is the spoken remark—meaning that not only is there a potentially real person, but he or she is *someone who can speak*, which means there's probably another person around, maybe in some room, or out in a field, an urgent but as yet undefined emotion building between them. It took me a long time to get a person with a name into one of my poems, and even longer to realize that I could use dialogue. People can talk in poems, just as they do in stories! It really was a kind of revelation.

Every assignment is the opportunity for some kind of unforeseen revelation, or (to use a more appropriately modest word) discovery. This assignment is a little anthology of such possibilities—a series of small provocations. Any one of them can be cleverly finessed, should the student be so inclined, but then the teacher can point out that inclination. Other students may stumble half-aware toward a singular voice and definite listener, the possibility of narrative and character, and actual *things* (like that piece of clothing), and creatures, because what poem can't be improved by allowing a dog into it? (And maybe the dog also has a name, is wearing a red bandana, and has recently—and strangely—arrived from Portugal.)

The most common danger of this assignment is not that it results in disconnected fragments, but that the students press the material too quickly toward coherence. They're so eager for things to make sense, and for everything to be finished. What I'm looking for here is not a substantial first draft, but one or two intriguing moments, so that I can say: Look, isn't this sentence much more compelling than anything else in your poem? So what if it doesn't make sense. It might. Try taking it out, setting the rest of what you have aside, and seeing where that one gesture might lead you. Try having nothing in mind but what might come next, which you can't know until you've written it. Try imagining without an end in mind. Try imagining that you'll get one if you find the right words to take you there.

Many Demands or a Dog, a Bear, or a Wolf

This assignment has many specific demands, designed not to constrain you so much as to free you to write lines that are interesting, surprising, and evocative in and of themselves. Consequently, don't worry too much—or too quickly—about what the poem might *mean*. Making sense is not your first task here; making exciting language is.

Here, then, is what the poem must do.

1. It must begin with one of the following lines:

   You might come here Sunday on a whim,

   I dreamed that in a city dark as Paris

   The first of the undecoded messages read:

   In Italy, where this sort of thing can occur,

Now it is only hours before you wake,

Should I get married? Should I be good?

I must explain why it is that at night, in my own house,

On the secret map the assassins

2. It must include at least four metaphors or similes.

3. It must be between twenty and twenty-five lines long.

4. It must be written in complete sentences.

5. It must contain all of the following: the name of a country; the first name of a person; a piece of clothing; one spoken remark (in quotation marks); and a dog, a bear, or a wolf.

Note: The first lines are from poems in the Mark Strand anthology. It's probably best to resist reading those poems while you're working on this assignment.

SUSAN RICH

COMMENTS ON MY NAME IS STAN AND I LOATHE LOBSTER: A POEM OF EXAGGERATION

There is no love more sincere than the love of food.
– George Bernard Shaw

I first created this exercise when confronted with sixty people who had shown up for what I thought would be a small afternoon workshop at Lower Columbia College in Longview, Washington. I was floored by the over-stuffed classroom and needed a fun way for people to introduce themselves to the group. Since we would be looking at the interconnections between poetry and food, I had everyone introduce themselves with one sentence that began with their name and then mentioned a food they either loved or loathed. Going around the very large circle provided a diversity of foods and expressions. I was amazed at how passionately and confidently people were when they spoke of their own personal preferences. It was a simple step from those first introductions to poems that expanded on the students' original sentences.

My hope is that this allows students to develop confidence in their writing, coupled with a sense of play (go wild; make chocolate your reason to live; would you die rather than eat chopped liver again?) so that they can create energetic and entertaining pieces.

My Name is Stan and I Loathe Lobster: A Poem of Exaggeration

Ask students to introduce themselves by giving their name and a food that they love or loathe. Once everyone has done this and you've perhaps asked a few questions—"Jeannine, why do you love sauerkraut?" or "Barry, what is there to loathe about chocolate ice cream"? —go to the activity below.

Write a poem in which you take your like or dislike to the level of the absurd. One woman in my workshop started with "I'm Karen and I love wild salmon." In her poem of exaggeration the wild salmon became a very sexy boyfriend waiting for her when she came home from work. Of course, once the poem gets going, the first line that we began with often becomes obsolete. Although you may also choose to keep a first line like this one, again, from my workshop: "There should be a law against a cheese smarter than me."

Have fun.

EMILY ROSKO

COMMENTS ON THE ACTIVATED VOICE

How does poetry differ from the prose of fiction? It's a perennial question that I ask my students—one that has an obvious first answer: a poem is organized in lines, whereas prose is not. But what makes a poem—a good poem—different from prose chopped up into lines? The trickier answer here: voice.

Unlike fiction, a poem does not need narrative scaffolding or an established character in order to speak. The speaker of a poem is immediate. The minute there is language in a poem we are plunked down in a lyric consciousness—an "I," a voice already made present. The lyric poem is all voice, and so a poem needs to convince us that a speaker is intimately present, even if we enter the poem not yet knowing the speaker's identity or situation. It is through voice—its chosen language and tone—that we come to understand the context from which the poetic speaker speaks. The poem, then, requires an activated voice that leaps up out of the silent, dead words on the page and is heard and animated by us as we read. One other way to think about a poem's voice, as Jorie Graham has written, is that it should feel as though, "it has battled a worthy opponent and has been gagged by it" (165). Though it might seem extreme to suggest that a poem is what survives our gagging on—our being overpowered by—experience, it captures the sense in which the words of the poem are the hard-fought, hard-won words. They are the residue of some struggle with some thing—experience, beauty, or pain.

The Activated Voice

The poem's first line is critical for establishing an activated voice, but, of course, a certain level of intimacy and urgency needs to be intoned throughout the poem. Graham is helpful again for understanding how we might achieve this. She asks us to think of the poem as "an act which could, very well, be the last act. It must feel that way—the very last act or the very first" (169). Imagine how you might sound if you were wavering on the risk of being harmed or in danger; or, if you were teetering on the edge of being saved or in astonishment. That is the voice of the lyric poem—an activated voice.

Take a look at this example of a first line from a novice poet:

As I was walking by, I thought I saw an old friend, but up close what I saw was not an old friend but a weary woman.

The line is lifeless, full of exposition. In a poem, there is no need to set up the poetic speaker with a phrase such as "I thought." This line can be turned from a static voice of self-narration to an activated voice that enacts its happening. Consider this revision:

An old friend?—No—a woman worn.

Here, all the extraneous prose is removed in order to situate the poem immediately in a lyric consciousness—a brain that is thinking: Did I just see an old friend? and which then answers itself, No, I saw another woman, and she looked worn out by life. The concision of the language matches the quickness of how a mind speaks to itself. Does it matter that we know the poetic speaker is "walking by" as in the first draft of this sentence? No, not really. As readers of poetry we can intuit this. What matters is that the poem's language enacts the situation of the encounter and how the speaker feels—taken aback abruptly and confused by what s/he are seeing.

Here are some strategies that activate poetic voice:

Direct Address
The use of "you"—or whether in the form of a pronoun, an term of endearment, or a proper name—is an easy, yet profound way to activate poetic voice. If someone turns and speaks to you, or calls you by name, you

tend to listen and respond. Direct address to a "you" in a poem gathers us all together, it places each one of us within the poem's lyric consciousness, as one scholar says, "You tends to hail; it calls everyone and everything by their inmost name" (Waters, 15). It works just as well to animate and personify things, as in Charles Simic's "Emily's Theme" which begins, "My dear trees, I no longer recognize you / In that wintery light" (5).

Conversational Diction

Words spoken in salutation ("Hello"), in affirmation ("Yes"), in negation ("No"), in consolation ("There there"), along with other conversational diction, such as colloquial expressions, give sound to active voicing. Vernacular phrases give clues as well to a poetic speaker's identity, tone, and attitude. Wallace Stevens's "Negation" begins glibly, "Hi! The creator too is blind" setting us up with a jaunty-seeming poetic speaker who soon launches into a larger teleological complaint (82).

Interrogative Mode

Questions by their very nature seek an answer or a response of some kind. The best conversationalists know it is important to ask thoughtful questions of others. In a poem, questions bring that presenced sense of I am talking to you forward. Mary Oliver's "The Summer Day" begins ("Who made the world?") and ends ("Tell me, what is it you plan to do / with your one wild and precious life?") with questions in order to engage and to challenge us to re-evaluate our lives (94). Rhetorical questions ("Eh, why not?") can dramatize a poetic speaker's internal deliberations, making us privy to overhearing their thoughts.

Imperatives

Imperatives are commands to act or behave a specific way: "Look," "Close the book," "Stop," or "Shh." Leon Stokesbury's "Unsent Message to My Brother in His Pain," begins with two poignant, imploring imperatives, "Please do not die now. Listen" (85). Similar to questions in a poem, imperatives perk our ears: their orders speak directly to us, the readers, making the voice feel very near.

Speech Acts (Performative Utterances)

According to the philosopher J. L. Austin, the acts speakers perform when they make an utterance are called speech acts. A poem, as a whole, can be thought of as a speech act, for it uses voice to perform its drama and to incite a response in the reader. A poem that begins, "Do not love me, I warn you," has a voice that urges us to heed these words. By saying "I warn you," this poetic speaker is performing the very act of warning. Language that articulates things to do (i.e., "I promise you," "I apologize," and, "I bequeath the estate to my brother") as well as to assert things (i.e., "We swear allegiance" and "I proclaim you Queen of England") constitutes performative utterances. Questions and imperatives also fall under the category of speech acts.

Interjections

Language that interrupts discourse in an exclamatory manner embodies the poetic voice on the page. Examples of interjections include: "Wow!" "Ugh," "My God!" "Aha," or "Hot damn!" Joshua Clover's "The Nevada Glassworks" begins with an explosive, onomatopoeic interjection, "Ka-Boom! They're making glass in Nevada! / Figure August, 1953, / mom's 13, it's hot as a simile" to underscore the darkly comic tone and critical attitude of the poetic speaker as he imagines his mother growing up in the Atomic Age (1).

Apostrophe

A particularly charged and theorized interjection, the apostrophe ("O" or "Oh") signals a moment when the poetic speaker loses language. It is the intensified cry of woe or surprise or wonderment—a sound for when all words fail to articulate the feeling. At a funeral for a once larger-than-life cousin, "Oh oh. Too much. Too much," laments the poetic speaker in Gwendolyn Brooks's "The Rites for Cousin Vit" as she comes to terms with the idea of Vit being gone (109). Apostrophe also is related to direct address, for the apostrophe captures the moment, too, when a speaker suddenly stops in her/his discourse and turns to address pointedly some person or thing, either present or absent. Toward the end of James Wright's "To the Muse," the poetic speaker exhausted by his grief, finally summons the "you" by name, "Oh Jenny" (176). Critical theorist Jonathan Culler argues that the apostrophe is a powerful tool in lyric poetry because it makes "a 'timeless present' [...] a special temporality which is the set of all moments at which writing can say 'now'"(149). Which is to say, apostrophe enacts the poem's happening, as though the poem's discourse and emotion were happening right now. Apostrophe is radically powerful in a poem, as well, because it can make an absence present. In Wright's poem, the speaker always will be overwhelmed by his grief ("Oh Jenny"), always will turn toward and address Jenny: the last possible way to bring her back.

Punctuation

Punctuation can help produce effects for how a poetic voice should be heard on the page. In our conversational discourse, we do not always speak eloquently. Sometimes we trip on our words, hesitate, stutter, lose track of what we are saying, fall silent, or become interrupted, and punctuation in a poem should strive to represent these imperfections of speech. The use of ellipses, for example, can represent a voice that trails off.

Parentheses, as an aside, can suggest a poetic speaker who might be second-guessing what s/he are saying. In Elizabeth Bishop's well-known last stanza of "One Art," the parentheticals voice the speaker's internal grappling and final admittance that she has been fooling herself, that there is no way to master the loss of a loved one:

Even losing you (the joking voice, a gesture
I love) I shan't have lied. It's evident
the art of losing's not too hard to master
though it may look like (Write it!) like disaster (178).

Parentheses also can function to break the fourth wall, similar to actors on a stage who turn from the drama's action to address the audience with their thoughts.

The em dash, similar to parentheses, is a versatile tool and it is best used to create the sense of an unstable poetic voice or of a voice breaking off. Bishop's child-speaker in "In the Waiting Room," has a moment of self-correction as she tries to understand others outside of herself: "Without

thinking at all / I was my foolish aunt, / I—we—were falling, falling"
(160). Additionally, an em dash can represent aposiopésis (falling silent)
exceedingly well; for example: "You better do what I say or else I'll—".

Lack of punctuation can offer interesting voice effects, too. A prime
example, Frank O'Hara's "Poem [Lana Turner has collapsed!]," with the
exception of two exclamation points, is punctuation-less. The absence of
punctuation reinforces the poetic speaker's excitable, hurrying manner of
speech so that the whole poem remains on the edge of suddenness:

I was trotting along and suddenly
it started raining and snowing
and you said it was hailing
but hailing hits you on the head
hard so it was really snowing and
raining and I was in such a hurry" (449).

The poetic speaker, in recounting these events leading up to the Lana Turner
headline, becomes breathless, near collapse himself.

Syntax
In general, carefully crafted syntax keeps any form of writing interesting,
and good writers know they should vary their sentence structures to
avoid formulaic, repetitive patterns (ARTICLE + NOUN + VERB +
PREPOSITIONAL PHRASE). In a poem, syntax embodies the poetic
speaker's state of mind. Inversion can imbue a voice with a sense that what is
being said is difficult to articulate, as in Gregory Orr's lines from "A Litany,"
"I remember someone hung from a tree near the barn / the deer we'd killed
just before I shot my brother" (18). Instead of saying the deer someone
hung from a tree near the barn, the poetic speaker recounts the memory
in a muddled manner, "someone hung from a tree near the barn," which
confronts us with a ghastly first image of death and enacts how painful it is
to tell what happened. Sentence fragments, in part because of the sudden
stop a period supplies, can offer jarring effects, enlivening the poetic voice's
articulation of the difficult emotional or psychological state.

Deixis

Deictic words are pointing words, which gesture to the time, place, or situation in which a speaker is speaking. Three main types are: (1) personal deixis includes pronouns of reference such as "you," "my," "ours," "us"; (2) spatial deixis includes "here" and "there" or "this," "that," "these," and "those"; and (3) temporal deixis includes "now," "then," "today," and "soon." Deictic language seems obvious and simple, but it supplies a poem with a complexity that is often taken for granted. Consider this first line: "Even now this landscape is assembling" from Louise Glück's "All Hallows" (61). Here, it is as though we enter a scene where all the pieces are gathering together, all the players are rushing into the frame. The poetic voice's declarative statement—"this landscape is assembling"—is full of knowingness and a charged, almost eerie aura. "Even now" does not simply indicate the moment when Glück penned the line, just as "this landscape" does not simply indicate the place where she wrote the poem. "Now" and "this" point to a context—the moment and place of our reading—and it creates the effect that the poem is presently happening. As with the use of apostrophe, deixis allows the poetic voice to become timeless, placeless, able to sing of any possible nows and any possible landscapes. Deixis activates poetic voice and makes a voice continually sound as though it is speaking directly to every one of us.

EXERCISE:

Write a poem using as many of these strategies as possible to create an activated voice. Approach this poem as though it were the "final act"—a poem of goodbye or last words.

Works Cited

Austin, J. L. *How to Do Things with Words*, 2nd ed. Boston, MA: Harvard University Press, 1975.

Bishop, Elizabeth. *The Complete Poems, 1927-1979*. New York, NY: Farrar, Straus and Giroux, 1999.

Brooks, Gwendolyn. *The World of Gwendolyn Brooks*. Harpercollins, 1971.

Clover, Joshua. *Madonna anno domini*. Baton Rouge, LA: Louisiana State University Press, 1997.

Culler, Jonathan. "Apostrophe." *The Pursuit of Signs*. Ithaca: Cornell University Press (1981). 135-54.

Glück, Louise. *The First Four Books of Poems.* New York, NY: Ecco Press, 1999.

Graham, Jorie. "Some Notes on Silence." *By Herself: Women Reclaim Poetry,* ed. Molly Mc-
  Quade. Saint   Paul, MN: Graywolf Press, 2000. 165-71.

O'Hara, Frank. *The Collected Poems of Frank O'Hara,* ed. Donald Allen. Berkeley, Ca: Univer-
  sity of
  California Press, 1995.

Oliver, Mary. *New and Selected Poems.* Boston, MA: Beacon Press, 1992.

Orr, Gregory. *The Caged Owl: New and Selected Poems.* Copper Canyon Press, 2002.

Simic, Charles. *Walking the Black Cat.* San Diego, CA: Harcourt Brace & Company, 1996.

Stevens, Wallace. *Collected Poetry and Prose.* New York, NY: The Library of America, 1997.

Stokesbury, Leon. *Autumn Rhythm: New and Selected Poems.* University of Arkansas Press,
  1996.

Waters, William. *Poetry's Touch: On Lyric Address.* Ithaca, NY: Cornell University Press, 2003.

Wright, James. *Above the River: The Complete Poems.* University Press of New England, 2000.

NATASHA SAJÉ

COMMENTS ON DRIVING STUDENTS TO THE DICTIONARY—EXERCISING ETYMOLOGY

The English language is lexically rich because of its history. When the Norman French invaded England in 1066, French became the language of the court and the ruling class, and Germanic-based Old English was relegated to "the common people." For a period of 400 years, English responded to the French influx via variance in spelling and by using different letters to make the same sound ("sew/so"), but most obviously by expanding its vocabulary. By Shakespeare's time, English had absorbed many Latin and Greek words by assimilation. When Samuel Johnson wrote his dictionary in 1755, he was attempting to standardize what had already become an unruly—or gloriously rich—language, infused with new words prompted by colonization, exploration, and technology. When English came to the new world, it was further enriched by Native American words like canoe and moccasin. Although English—like French, German, and Italian—has Indo-European roots, its diction is less pure and more interesting because synonyms have roots in both the Anglo-Saxon and the Latinate/Greek, and because it has absorbed "new world" words. A writer can often choose between these "families" to achieve a particular effect; "inculcate" and "masticate," for example, are different from "teach" and "chew."

Until our era, most writers learned Latin and Greek and had training in the history and structure of English, and in etymology. Even William Blake, who was not trained in classical languages, taught himself enough about Latin and Greek to use the devices of etymology in his poems. Times have changed, however. While 41% of high school students study a foreign language, only 1.5% of that group study Latin, much less Greek. This means that most contemporary readers must make a conscious effort to learn etymology by looking up words in a dictionary that lists word roots. The etymology of a word can deepen the meaning of a poem by carrying an image, for instance the root of "cross" in "crucial" or the root of "star" in "consider." Understanding word origins helps readers understand their buried or historical meanings as well as see the amplifying images they carry with them. *This exercise drives students to the dictionary in an attempt to foster a more precise use of words as well as build knowledge of word origins.*

Driving Students to the Dictionary—Exercising Etymology

Open a dictionary with etymologies, such as American Heritage or the Oxford English dictionary, at random, and skim the page until you get to a word whose root you didn't know. Begin a poem tracing the history of the word back to its root image. Take detours along the way: the goal is play! Alternately, you may create a false etymology for a word, as do Elizabeth Alexander's "Affirmative Action Blues," Allen Grossman's "Sentinel Yellowwoods," and Gjetrud Schnackenberg's "Supernatural Love."

*Examples: Donald Bogen's "Necklace" and "Bullhorn"; Sharon Bryan's "Body and Soul"; Robert Hass's " Etymology"; Kevin McFadden's "Faith-Coated Treaties" and "Credit, Check"; Campbell McGrath's "Zeugma"; Heather McHugh's "Etymological Dirge"; Susan Mitchell's "Golden Fleece," "Love Song," and "Self Portrait with Young Eros"; Natasha Sajé's "Creation Story," "Appetites," and "Water Music"; Gary Snyder's *Mountains and Rivers without End.*

SAMPLE POEM

Creation Story

Vanilla
is the Emily Dickinson of orchids:
plain white flowers, yet its lush vine
can trail ten stories carried by the trees.
Green pods are cured dark walnut brown.
Sliced open lengthwise: infinitesimal seeds,
printer's ink. Their black flecks ice cream
or a sauce for pheasant or steeps in oil

where the scent lingers, like a morning moon.
The Aztecs used vanilla, brewed it salty for Columbus.
It took the English to make it sweet.
A cure for impotence, they thought,
smoking it with tobacco.
Cunt-struck, the Elizabethans said, when
drawn by a woman's scent
or the way she moved her head,
they wanted her more than words.
From the Spanish, *vainilla*,
diminutive of Latin, *vagina*,
the term for sheath.
A vagina becomes a case—
a portico covering travelers,
a scabbard for a sword—
the way Ptolemy made the earth the center
and the Greeks named orchid tubers
after testicles.
No matter that some words glide over the tongue,
entice us with sweet stories,
we're still stuck
with their roots in our throats.

—Natasha Sajé

MARTHA SILANO

COMMENTS ON THANKFUL, SORT OF

I like this exercise because it flat-out rejects black and white thinking about God's benevolence. The assumptions that it's always good in a poem to give thanks, cultivate the attitude of gratitude, and to wax praise-fully are all called into question. (I won't argue that in real life it's best to be thankful and gracious, but in the life of poetry it's almost always more interesting to explore the range of feelings the word *God* evokes).

This exercise exercises the yin-yang muscles in our gray matter, where the almighty gray area resides. In this Nantucket-foggy place, it's okay to be unsure, ambivalent, querying, indignant—quite thankful, yes, but also quite outraged. When it works, this exercise assists students in avoiding well-trodden ground. Instead, it offers the less worn path of expressing both ebullient appreciation and stinging criticism. At its best it emboldens beginning poets to take risks with what they're willing to reveal about our cruel, yet miraculous universe.

Thankful, Sort Of

Begin by reading and discussing poems of praise and gratitude. Naomi Shihab Nye's poems are a good place to start. Pablo Neruda's odes are also worthy of study. Any poem where the speaker wants to kiss the floor in gratitude, but where there's no mention of God's apparent absence during, for instance, the Holocaust, will work just fine. Next it's time to explore poems that take pot-shots at God. The best ones address His Almighty, letting Him know just how pissed they are. Susan Browne's "Poem in My Mother's Voice," found in *The Poet's Companion* edited by Dorianne Laux and Kim Addonizio, is a superb example. Here's a brief excerpt:

When my mother meets God,
she says, *Where the hell have you been?*

Jesus Christ, don't you care about anyone
but yourself? It's time you wake up,
smell the coffee, shit or get off the pot.

Now students have two models in their heads: poems of intoxicating
thankfulness and those that question the 100% belief in God's benevolence.
Now all they have to do is smoosh the two together and see what happens.
In a workshop or small group peer review, students and the instructor
provide encouragement to push draft poems toward increasing specificity,
startling metaphorical leaps, and even wilder swinging between abject wrath
and merciful appreciation. They can start in positive territory and wind up
cautionary, or they might find themselves beginning in ambivalence and
ending in acceptance. Or, best of all, they can aim to perch their speaker
smack dab in the middle of the see saw.

SAMPLE POEM

Thankful Quite Thankful

for the thin clear soup
the old man who shuffles along
as if he might be carrying
in that steamy bowl
all our children's futures

for this and for the chicken
the blood that swirled
the cook who peeled
the forty cloves

don't tell me you've
been oversleeping
all your subscriptions expired
and no access to cable

actually I bet you couldn't
balance a checkbook
I mean if humanity were a Fortune 500
we'd've fired you a couple millennia ago

none of us ever did like the prima donnas
who show up for weddings
but where are they when you need
for instance help with moving?

spider webs and the crab nebulae aside
what sort of comfort are cooing doves
the half-honk half-squeak of herons?
Thankful quite thankful

for the suctioned legs of an octopus
that color like a bruise
for Superglue and the woman
who served up (grumpily
with a few swift thwacks)

the best pizza in all Sicily
praise the lawn
boisterous with beetles
praise the wide windows
out of which we see

the Hing Loon restaurant
though mostly this thin clear soup
this bowl so carefully

—Martha Silano

PHILIP TERMAN

COMMENTS ON THE JOKE POEM

Even for those who have read nonsense poems and parodies (such as "Jabberwocky" and well-wrought light verse) as children, especially (but not only) beginning creative writing students assume that poetry has to be "difficult," and if it has to be difficult, it also has to be "serious." But of course in introducing writers to the thrills of poetry writing, we ask them to write about what many of us like to write about—our personal lives. Even there, though, students often turn to the "big" issues of death and loss. For some reason, we sometimes believe that if it's not depressing, it's not poetry. Naturally, we know better: humor, whether it be in the form of satire or puns, is necessary for poetry. We've read Shakespeare's bawdy songs, Philip Larkin's satiric turns, Theodore Roethke's adult-appealing "children's verse," ee cummings, and—to bring it up to date—Billy Collins.

The Joke Poem

One simple way to introduce humor into a poetry workshop is to write a poem around a joke, or jokes. Jokes are good to use because, besides their natural attention-getting quality, virtually everyone has heard and can remember at least one. The poem should not only include the joke or a reference to it, but use narration in sharing the "origin" of the joke—when and how you first heard it. (A grandparent? A friend?) What was the context, setting? In a bar? Around a campfire? Does the joke reveal anything interesting about the teller (probably the "real" subject of the poem)? Of course, very few jokes are "original," and thus a joke will reflect not only the teller, but can reveal a larger context that can reflect many qualities, such as race, class, time-period, linguistic style.

When I assign a "Joke Poem," I have students divide into groups of three or four, and simply have them share jokes with each other to stimulate ideas. It's certainly a fun way to start. Sometimes the poems reflect this sense of "fun," and the joke poem provides us with a poetic reflection of a fond memory. Often, though, the poems that result go beyond the surface 'humor' with which we started into deeper associations of the speaker's relationship to the "teller" —humor, as it often does, opening into deeper poignancies. Significantly, the 'joke' need not be a good one. The point is *Can remembering the joke lead into deeper poetic sources?*

SAMPLE POEM

Here's an example of a poem I wrote that ends with a small grim joke, one my father liked to tell, though in the poem the context influenced me to do some alteration. I didn't think about the joke until I suddenly remembered it at the very end of the writing process, and it seemed an appropriate way to end a poem about how we associate visual reminders (in this case, seeing the time "11:11" on a digital clock) with people we've loved and lost.

11:11

Uncanny, how often I look
at the digital clock flaring: 11:11,

a symmetry of ones, lines reaching
toward the sky, down into the earth—

the date my father died, veteran
that he was, in the great war,

the last one, they say, worthy
of the fight, and then the aftermath:

wife and four sons, the daily grind
of coffee and work and supper: 11:11,

reminding me of him, of something

he wants me to accomplish in his name,

saying, in the repetition of our loneliest
number: *I'm still here*, the number

out of which all other numbers arise:
one and one and one and one, what

some say the Lord is and what we remain
despite our efforts to lose ourselves in another,

what is divisible by only itself: 11:11,
a family of selves, each a single entity—

perhaps that, each of us is one more
than nothing—is that it?—the message

you send, from wherever you are, into time?
Or is the first of our infinity of odd numbers

just another one of your jokes, which
I'm reminded of when I'm reminded of you:

It's 11:11, and you're pushing up daisies.

—Philip Terman

PHILIP TERMAN

COMMENTS ON THE NEST POEM

How do long poems get written? Often they get written by assembling, shaping, and arranging together a lot of shorter pieces. This technique can be especially effective for a "sectional" poem—a poem consisting of many shorter pieces that are associated through a larger theme. Sometimes these "associations" are direct; often they are indirect, metaphorical, imaginative. Think of a collage. Think of a nest built with bits of bird feather, hay strands, dog hair. The nest is what they have in common.

The Nest Poem

Write in your journals every day (hopefully at least a page) for a period for at least two or, better, three weeks, and, during that time, do not go back to what you've written. After this period, return to all those pages, and, at your computer, type up any words, phrases, or interesting pieces of language that your writing produced that seem similar to each other. Is there an image and/or an incident that recurs? To paraphrase Richard Hugo, the person who wrote a line on Tuesday will be the same person who writes a line on Thursday—there must be some connection between those lines. Sometimes the connections are indirect, but often they are direct— our minds will reproduce what situations, incidents, memories, etc., that are occupying our attention. Furthermore, since our minds automatically want to make connections, while in the process of "culling" from the original journal pages, we will consciously or unconsciously add, delete, change, i.e. shape—responding to what has been composed in the moment of composition.

In reality, when I attempt to write this kind of poem, I'll go through a journal (or journals) that cover a much larger period of time; obviously, a semester course won't allow for that to happen, and the purpose of this assignment is to simply give you a taste of how a long poem might get written. It's important for the serious poetry student to understand that language can generate itself, and by following its course we can make discoveries that can lead us into a more ambitious poem.

If one thinks of the poem as a nest, then it "loosens up" the rules of what we can put into it. It can incorporate small pieces of narrative, surreal imagery, bits of prose, even "non-poetic" material like cooking recipes (see Robert Hass' "Songs to Survive the Summer"), as long as they are all held together by something: a theme (in the Hass poem, the death of a neighbor) or a common association (see Li-Young Lee's poem, "Dreaming of Hair").

SAMPLE POEM

Here's a "collage poem" of short sections all related by the season—Fall, and the Jewish sacred Holiday period called the "Days of Awe," in which it is believed that one can "turn" away from one's previous sins in the process of healing and spiritual growth.

The Turning

Yellow-as-sunlight Jerusalem artichokes,
Hefty hydrangeas, white-to-pink—

Time scatters us into the powder
The milkweed floats after grinding it
Between two fingers.
    *

If we had to choose,
We'd live forever. Because *to be*
Is the only verb we know.
    *

There's a tree within the tree
The light reaches deeper into,
Where we are uncertain about our lives--

The jeweled apples, the wind-rustlings--
These spectaculars
Asserting their authority over whatever heartache
Was breaking us.

> *

Time for awe and the seasonal decay,
For penitents to sway like these cornstalks
In the intermittent wind, time for casting off
The withered heart.

Time for speechlessness.

> *

Time for the red-tailed hawk to float
Toward the sharp red and yellow leaves,
Leading us to conclusions:

Summer held its own,
The inevitabilities
Of longing, the children's laughter under
The loud stars.

> *

Migrating birds, what wisdom?

Season us with your autumn,
Its glorious summation,
Its desire that is a desire of embers,
Our bodies the bread the earth will eat.

> *

I climb the ladder
For the last of the apples,

Higher and higher
With the thought of cider, picking

Each one within reach, stepping out
Onto the thinnest branches

For the difficult ones,
The obscure ones, the ones

Concealing themselves
In their darkest cluster of leaves--

Forgetting the height,
How close my death.
            *
Not like Frost, not overtired,
I shake the limbs into a green hail-swirl.

Bella—six and in the flush of her enthusiasms
Of her enthusiasms—chases
And gathers and tosses them

Into the wheelbarrow, the summer-into
Autumn sun perched in the crotch
Of the tree.

It's the Day of Atonement.

This is not a synagogue
And we are not beating our breasts,

Our sins spread out like this ripe fruit
We'll simmer down on the stove for sauce,

In this harvest we desired.
            *
To think

Of this beauty occurring without us,

Like the last glimpse of the swallows
As they disappear
Into their next chronicler,

The days equipped for flight.

*

To consider the apple tree--

To know that devotion,
That mission to blossom
And therefore fruit and fall
And be part of the larger earth.

*

A peck of the last of the remnants
Left too long on the porch,
Monument to our abundance.

We haven't the heart to eat them,
Reminders of the bounty our lives were,
As we waited beneath, shook the limbs
And scattered the children.

*

We are becoming our nothing,
Save for the shadows
The apple tree shapes across this page,

Our lives a preparation for permanence.

We're thinning out into the pure moment,
Listening to the wind's voice saying:

We can find a way to live.

We can be inscribed in the book.
We can have a place to store our griefs.

Turn, it said.
Turn to the beauty
That will outlast your sorrow.

—Philip Terman

PHILIP TERMAN

COMMENTS ON THE HERITAGE POEM

Though America is filled with ethnic poets, whose heritage/culture informs a great deal of their work (one thinks of the Palestinian-American Naomi Shihab Nye, the Chinese-American Li-Young Lee, the Native-American Sherman Alexie, and so many others), there is a paucity of poetry exercises that draw creative writing students' attention to the possibilities of this subject. One can draw a wide interpretation with the term "heritage." Though often seen as ethnic, heritage can include race, gender, religion, the area where the student grew up, or any kinds of rituals associated with heritage.

The Heritage Poem

In this exercise, consider your ancestry (or, in some cases, lack of ancestry, which could also produce intriguing possibilities), language (words and phrases passed down), objects, clothing, humor, attitudes, physical characteristics, food, etc. Of course, heritage and cultural background play a more significant role for some than for others. As I mentioned earlier, though, often what we perceive we "lost" or "lack" can open up areas for poetry (sometimes painful ones). The assignment provides an excuse for us to become more informed about our ancestral background: I encourage doing a "roots search" (interviewing parents and grandparents would be a good place to start) to learn more about where they came from.

The goal is not to simply write "another ethnic" poem that appeals to only that group it refers to; rather, references to heritage and culture are, like other tropes and symbols, "windows" into deeper, more universal subjects that all readers might respond to. We look into the human through any of our particular cultural windows.

SAMPLE POEM

Here's an example of one of my own poems that I include to show that writing about heritage/culture can also provide opportunities for humor. Part of thinking about "identity" is our natural (and poetic) impulse to satirize and parody:

Putzing Around
After Neruda

It happens that I'm tired of being a Jew.
It happens that I go into synagogues shriveled up.
I stroll around the Jewish Community Center
singing "Hava Nagila" in falsetto.
The smell of my mother's challa makes me sob out loud.
I want nothing but the repose of barbequed pork or shellfish,
I want to see no more maps of Israel, nor mazuzas,
nor Stars of David, nor fancy kabalistic necklaces.
It happens that I'm tired of my facial hair and my sideburns.
It happens I'm tired of being a Jew.
Just the same it would be delicious
to scare a Wasp with a yarmulke
or knock a nun dead with one slap of my t'fillin.
It would be beautiful
to go through the streets with a kosher knife
kibitzing until they crucify me.
I do not want to go on being a Talmudic nudnic,
kvetching, atoning, davening in the sanctuary.
I do not want to be the inheritor of so much guilt, stiff-necked.
For this reason, Leviticus infects us all,
with its strictures and restrictions,
howling its Jehovah.
I want to visit the houses of the gentiles,
certain bakeries smelling of lard,

streets full of shiksas begging for my attention.
There are Jewish mothers beckoning from doors
of the houses which I hate,
statues of their adored sons on the suburban lawns,
stuffed ancestors displayed above the couch,
and holy tchotchkes from Jerusalem all over the place.
It happens that I'm tired of being a Jew.

—Philip Terman

ANTONIO VALLONE

COMMENTS ON FILLER UP

Most newspapers survive by a distortion of *The New York Times* motto. Instead of "All the news that's fit to print," it's all the news that fits we print. So, as copy editors work full-length news stories around the advertisements their newspapers need to stay in print, sometimes a need is created for fillers—short, quirky news stories to take up white space.

Those fillers can easily become fodder for writers. You can find fillers just about anywhere: mainstream newspapers, supermarket tabloids, on television, or online. My taste leans toward religious fillers, but they can be found on just about any topic. They can feed our imaginations and help us toward all the poetry that's fit to print.

Filler Up

I have a sudden story, "Freezer Jesus," that appeared in *Sudden Stories: The MAMMOTH Book of Miniscule Fiction,* edited by Dinty W. Moore. My story was based on a "filler" about a man who saw the image of Jesus on the side of a freezer he kept on the porch of his trailer. I had successfully used the filler for years in creative writing classes before I wrote my story based on it. Then, at a reading I gave in upstate New York, I learned from a fan of John Dufresne's that Dufresne had written a short story called "The Freezer Jesus," based on the same filler and published in his collection *The Way that Water Enters Stone.* Dufresne also turned his story into a screenplay that was made into a film by the same title and released in 2003.

Though I've given two examples of fiction, using fillers can help produce poetry equally well. I've discovered that confinement in many forms can help writers. As Richard Wilbur said, "The strength of the genie comes from being in a bottle." With my National University MFA students, many of them taking a poetry class as their required second genre, simply limiting them to a certain number of lines can help them keep what I call the "blah,

blah, blah" out of their poems. With introductory creative writing students, fillers can help them discover the need for images, as I usually require them to fill in the filler with details, which I often specify. For example, in a filler I often use now, a news story called "Two Eggs Over Jesus," I have them name the cook who sees Jesus in the bottom of the pan, name the waitress, name the diner, create all the details of their poem's dramatic situation: the who, what, where, when, why, and how of the poem. It's fun to hear their poems alone and in comparison to what other students wrote. For some students, these filler-prompted poems are often their best of the semester. The exercise, then, is to use these fillers or find your own and then write a poem or two around them.

ANTONIO VALLONE

COMMENTS ON ODES TO SIMPLE THINGS

Sometimes, the imaginations of beginning poetry writers are clouded with so many convoluted and misperceived notions about poetry that a lesson in simplicity—the *art* of being simple—is what they need first. I might have students read Ted Kooser and Mary Oliver, both deceptively simple. I might select some other poets who are on my radar at the time. Most often, I choose an ode by Pablo Neruda.

Odes to Simple Things

My favorite of Neruda's myriad odes is "Ode to My Socks." It helps students see just how simple they can be and still have a poem. Who, after all, doesn't own a pair of socks? Find one of the many copies of Neruda's ode on-line and read it. Then write your own ode to something simple but evocative in your life.

The art of being simple is timeless: Shaker furniture, the little black dress (especially with Audrey Hepburn in it), the ode to simple things. Desirable simplicity.

SAMPLE POEM

Here is a poem written by my son, John Vallone, when he was in a member of Young Publishers' Club at the DuBois Area Middle School:

Forced Ode to My Sharpies

Two Ziploc bags
Of markers
Inside my room.
Sharpie brand,

Both thick and thin tip,
Some double pointed,
Some capped, some like clicky pens.
All the colors in the universe;
Red, Dark and Light Blue, Yellow,
Purple (and Purple), a rare Grey.
And all of the Greens you can think of.
I'll uncap one, and start to draw
Whatever comes to me:
The planet Texanna Prime, in a far-off arm of the galaxy.
Earth 9999, populated by cyborg mold zombies.
Reptilia, the alternate universe of lizards, snakes, and dragons.
All these places and more;
Hard to believe that whole worlds
Live inside these tiny markers.
Hard to believe that this poem is a world,
And my parents forced me to create it.

—John Vallone

* John loves to draw, and Sharpies, if not always poetry, are part of his everyday life. Though you won't be able to see it in this book, he even made the names of the colors the actual colors using his imagination and our color printer.

ANTONIO VALLONE

COMMENTS ON THROW ME A LIFE LINE

Students of all ages, like anyone wallowing in any sea, even a sea of poetry, appreciate a life line.

Throw Me a Life Line

On my way to do a poetry reading at Ohio University Lancaster, I drove along a stretch of highway where the only radio station I could tune in clearly was all-rap format. So, by myself and without any other choice, I listened. One of the raps I heard was "21 Questions" by 50 Cent. The rap contained a line I really loved: "I love you like a fat kid loves cake," which I used to prompt a poem. (Without a pen or pencil and paper handy, I misremembered the line as "I love you more than a fat kid loves cake," so that's the way it appears in my poem. My apologies to 50 Cent.)

Baked Goods

"I love you more than a fat kid loves cake."
50 Cent, great philosopher of the 21st century,
understands his baked goods. For his own sake,
I hope he knows as much about love. Myself,

I was a fat kid once. I loved my cake
and ate it, too. In its absence, I dreamt about icing,
shoving my hands wrist-deep into its sugary lake,
pulling out layers by the handfuls, crumb bling.

In its presence, I cut slices heart-big.
I forked in chunks to overfill my mouth. I licked
my fingertips, the fork, plate, and table, erasing
riffs of butter cream I understood no better than hieroglyphs.

The whole experience inspired me to give students a line to work off of.
I've used this prompt in Young Publishers' Club, a writing group I have run
for four years at the DuBois Area Middle School, and in my introductory
poetry writing classes at Penn State DuBois. It's an exercise that has helped
produce many fine and funny poems. Here it is:

Use this line to write a poem of your own. And as a follow-up exercise,
see if you can find other "life lines" to borrow, write after, and share with
others.

CHARLES HARPER WEBB

COMMENTS ON FUSION EXERCISE

I like this exercise because it guarantees that poets will write about things that matter to them, and it forces poets to look at these things in ways that are new to them, finding connections they did not suspect before. Writing the poem becomes an act of discovery, which may give rise to poems that are complex yet clear, without a hint of "exercise" surrounding them. This exercise also displays the brain's amazing ability to make sense of almost anything.

Fusion Exercise

Choose two subjects that interest you—the more different and apparently unrelated, the better. You may choose two stories, two processes (making beer, lethal injections), a story and a process, whatever. The important thing is that both subjects be of real interest to you.

Now write a poem in which you combine the two subjects, letting each intermingle with and illuminate the other. Ideally, you will have no idea how the two interconnect until—it may seem like magic—they do.

SAMPLE POEM

Below is an example of this process from my own work. (Also, B.H. Fairchild's "In Czechoslovakia" from *Local Knowledge* is a wonderful example.)

The Mummy Meets Hot-Headed Naked Ice-Borers

Djedmaatesankh—temple musician, wife of Paankhntof,
daughter of Shedtaope—died childless, aged thirty-five,
in the tenth century B.C., of blood poisoning

from an abscessed incisor. CAT scans
of her mummy show how the abscess chewed
a walnut-sized hole in her upper jaw, gnawing

bone the way the creatures called "hot-headed
naked ice-borers" gnaw tunnels through
Antarctic ice. Six inches long, hairless and pink,
they look in pictures like sea lions with tumors
on their foreheads, and saber-teeth. The teeth
chew tunnels; the "tumors" are lumps of bone,

the skin of which writhes with blood vessels
radiating heat. Their normal temperature
is 110 degrees. Djedmaatesankh's fever
may have reached 104. One shot of penicillin
could have saved her, but it was 3000 years away.
Knowing about ice-borers might have saved French

explorer Philippe Poisson, who disappeared in 1837.
At five-foot-six, he could have been a large penguin:
the ice-borers' favorite food. A pack collects
under a penguin and, with their foreheads,
melts the ice it's standing on. The penguin sinks
as in quicksand; the borers attack like piranha,

leaving behind only beak, feathers, and feet—
as if the bird has taken them off before bed. Think
of Poisson, torn into fragments by their fangs.
Think of Djedmaatesankh in the three weeks the abscess
took to kill her. How did her husband feel,
hearing her scream? Watching her corpse carried

to the embalmers? Seeing the molded likeness
of her face rise from her pupal coffin? Did he weep

to lose his only love? Was he relieved
that he could remarry, and possibly have sons?
Or had mistresses provided those?
Did his wife's death make him curse, thank, cease

believing in his gods? Did Poisson's wife in Paris
dream of penguin beaks, feathers, feet encased
in ice? Did she see pink squirming things
with Phillipe's face? The first night Djedmaatesankh
went to bed with a toothache, did she dream
she was in a room crowded with people in strange clothes,

and while a white-skinned boy looked down at her
through a transparent wall like frozen air, making noises
that sounded like "Eeoo, gross," his sister began to scream,
and had to be carried outside, and that night
dreamed of Djedmaatesankh walking toward her,
gauze dripping from her shriveled, childless hands?

—Charles Harper Webb (© 1997)

CHARLES HARPER WEBB

COMMENTS ON SECRETS EXERCISE

I like this exercise because it steers writers away from their own point of view, forcing them to inhabit the mind of someone else, and thus escape the solipsistic rut into which it's so easy to fall. This can be exhilarating, and liberating. It also ensures at least some level of drama and conflict in produced poems, since a secret is no secret unless some drama surrounds it.

Secrets Exercise

First, ask someone to write out a secret, and give it to you. It can be the teller's own secret, or someone else's, or some combination of the two. It can be true, false, or partly true. The only restriction is that it should be told in a single sentence.

Using these same guidelines, write down a secret of your own.*

Now write a poem that either begins with the other person's secret, ends with the secret, or uses the secret as the subject for a poem. Let yourself stretch out, get wild, be adventurous, be shocking. Have fun! The object is to enter a mind different from your own.

This being said, I've found that sometimes writers surprise (and delight) themselves with the secrets they write. If you want to use your own secret, that's your right.

For an extra challenge, you can write a poem that combines the secrets, as in The Fusion Exercise earlier in this book.

Once you have a rough draft that seems promising, you're no longer "locked into" the secret in any way. Change the wording of the secret, or disregard it entirely if it no longer serves. Revise the poem as if it's entirely your own. It is.

*When this exercise is done in class, I ask everyone to write their secret twice: one copy to give to me, and one to keep. I collect everyone's secrets, place them in a sack, and have the students pick someone else's secret at random.

SAMPLE POEM

Here is an example of secrets worked into my own poetry. What the original secrets were is my secret.

Sneaker Males

Big Bo the Beetle digs a burrow under a prime heap
of howler monkey dung, fills it with females, then guards
the threshold, brandishing a horn as big as he is;
yet nub-nosed Sylvester tunnels into Bo's estate
and mounts Bo's females as His Enormosity does

the oblivious dance called I'm-The-One. So genes
of sneaker males survive. Tone deaf canaries.
Deer with pygmy racks. Cuttlefish so low on male
mystique they wear drab, female hues, mix with the Big
Gun's girls, then, when His Studliness turns

his rainbow-pulsing back, dart in to sneak some female
a packet of sperm. So every man is not six-nine
with a brick chin. My son, watching Smackdown
on TV, flexes and struts, then body-slams the teddy-
bear Grandma sent for cuddling. "You want

a piece of me?" he shrills, and leaps on Kid Bear
while I cringe. How long until Kid Bear is me?
If only God had made me Heavyweight Champ,
as I used to pray. Still, Tall Mike Ball, who dragged me
through Taft Junior High's halls in my jock-strap,

got shot to death robbing a liquor store. Dallas Brandt,
Waltrip High's All State tail back, sports a frog belly,
and runs a Laundromat, while I boast an Alpha job,

A-list wife, and All Star son because, years back,
like Sergeant Wimply of the Yukon, I failed to get my man.

He played guitar, had long blond hair and "connections"
(my girlfriend gushed) "to Aerosmith." "Just a friend,"
she claimed. But when her roommate said, "She's
at the library . . ." then stumbled over "studying," I slipped
my Boy Scout hatchet in my belt, and went hunting.

Back in high school, I'd played Astrologist, the better
to trade horoscopes with Cyndy P while Detective Daddy
grilled me from the den. Helping Marti N with algebra,
I encouraged her to whine about football heavy
Blake B, and felt her breasts when X would not

be found. That night, though, I prowled the stacks
like Bo, who's heard suspicious scuffling and, horn
buffed and ready, comes. Rage and pain had swollen me
to Alpha size when, sure I saw them, I yanked
my hatchet out. But the couple kissing in the dust

of British Lit were startled strangers. Nor did I find
the traitors in the parking lot, though I peered in
every car window before I drove home sobbing,
threw myself in bed, and woke next morning in the small,
familiar body I wear now.

—Charles Harper Webb (© 2007)

Poetry Anthology:

MAMMOTH BOOKS POETS

Vicky Anderson

❖

Sean Thomas Dougherty

❖

Jeff Grieneisen

❖

William Heyen

❖

Cynthia Hogue

❖

Henry Hughes

❖

Jeff Knorr

❖

Gerry LaFemina

Harriett Levin

❖

Scott Minar

❖

Jerry Mirskin

❖

Erin Murphy

❖

Liz Rosenberg

❖

Jeff Schiff

❖

John Stigall

❖

Phil Terman

VICKY ANDERSON

IN MEXICO, THE POSSIBILITY OF RESCUE

Ex-votos are paintings on wood, tin, or canvas
commemorating miraculous interventions

In this one a train wreck is averted.
In another a crudely painted ship lists
and is righted by Guadalupe,
who still makes time for small miracles:
an operating theatre, a bloodied leg
reattached, a child's bed approached by flames
that retreat in the lick of time, a *barracho*
yanked back from a tequila swigging devil.
And now the miracles become even smaller:
walking to the top of Cinco de Mayo
without breakage when the dozen
fresh eggs are offered in a sack,
or the miracle of the bee riding
a bran muffin all the way into
the fleshy cave of your mouth,
the miracle of its exit at the moment
of your exclamatory "Oh."
For hours your whole head buzzes
as if it caged hummingbirds.
This is the miracle of the body's memory
you tell yourself, and now you feel acutely alive.
The bee in question was weighted
with pollen and too sluggish to sting.
Spiraling out of your dark tunnel,
he was heady with second chances,
crowned with gratitude, reckless in flight
while quietly, miracles accumulate everywhere.

WHY I CANNOT SWIM

Because you asked, it could have been the large German
I had to swim towards in my first lesson and the depth

of the murky blue, the lens through which I could see
the tree trunk legs of the older, skirted swimmers.

Blue that was just another wall to keep me from
the unreachable laddered one. Or it could have been

the tight cap that yanked the hair from my scalp
and cut circulation to the part of my brain

that might have allowed me to float.
Back then I was known for my sinking.

I sunk faster and deeper than any suited child.
Later, boys liked holding me under

or sometimes holding me up
while my drowned girl hair fanned out around my face,

and sometimes gently, oh so gently, they'd let go
and I'd sink slowly, and those times I'd be ready to drown.

But I understand what the rest of you mean
when you speak about swimming.

Yes, I've been my own Ophelia, but I've had dreams
of rocketing through water like it was sky.

And sometimes in my swim dreams,
I can float both treading and supine, sometimes

my head-up crawl has a polar beauty
that brings even lifeguards to applause.

MY MOTHER AT TWENTY, SWIMMING

In 1943 when the U.S. ordered a 10% reduction of fabric
      in swimsuits, my mother bared her midriff and donned
           her bubble crepe rubber swim cap to move into

the cerulean blue of the township public pool.
      While she scissor-kicked her way from one end
           to the next, the young boys watched the engine

of her body propel her out of their small town reach.
      Towards what, she couldn't know. She had not yet created my father
           although he existed in some crude form, a handsome draft

of who he might be. She had not thought up the daughters
      to fill the empty dotted-Swiss dresses, ruffled and starched.
           Her future was safely tissued in a cedar chest,

her father still flesh, not yet relic, frame or box. She still had the distance
      to go, but first the tiled wall at the end of each lap, a blind feel
           then somersault. A push off and the next easy glide.

FLORIDA, 1963

girl in Jenny Lind bed   attic room
    into which heat rises

and settles   torpor   one room of
    air-conditioned comfort

in which to watch Kennedy shot
    again and again

downstairs the outline of a cat
    on a bed weighted

by heavy crochet   a neighbor ringing
    the doorbell cradling a thrush

your cat has killed my bird
    mother says God's bird

by way of correction   mother has never
    said God before

mother's mood lightens when the truck
    of rich grandmother things arrives

a chaise filled with down   girl may sit
    briefly and without indentation

downstairs Kennedy gets shot again
    and the maid whose husband was shot

but not like Kennedy   polishes
    the rich grandmother table

where women sit to smoke   by way
    of correction the girl goes to a friend's

apartment   rooms above a diner   diningroom
       opens to a tar roof

girls dance as pink boucle absorbs blood
       again and again

THE LANGUAGE OF STORMS

When it comes, it comes
      fast and frontal, and the boy
            chasers in whom storms

have been brewing for years
      shout the first spondees
            of warning: *cloud wall*

and then the husky
      three syllable *power flash*,
            urgently mouthed.

These are the boys who never
      loved words, mute boys
            whose lean bodies

and shiny cars were language enough,
      and now as the named ingredients
            percolate

(moisture, lift, and wind shear),
      the super cell forms.
            These Nebraska boys know

atmosphere and are ready to pronounce it now:
      rotation, rolling maelstrom,
            off the tongue, the vortex has begun.

STORM SERIES

I.
Some events leave their proof behind.
For that, we loved our tornado.
When the flying debris landed,
the whole dustbin landscape
was made of leavings.
The flattened farm 600 yards to our left
was testimony of our trial.
And the thing above the three of us
(you, me, and the black
dog who pissed herself)
was furious halo, made weightier
with each object lofted
into its fray.
There was no blessing, no benediction
to that promiscuous sky.

II.
Two states away, I still rake safety glass
from my hair. Here I've grown
suspicious of the sky's utter blueness.
Turbulence does not care for this place,
the absence of vorticity
is the only disturbance in town.

III.
It's who you almost die with that matters.
I've recently chosen well.
You lied in all the right places.
The black cloud is humming
with particles, the particles
mean no harm.
A storm is an address you inhabit briefly.
Your hand pushed my face
onto the floor of the truck.
Just the gravity I required.
The rest was confetti, a large
and circular parade, but roaring.

SEAN THOMAS DOUGHERTY

SEAN THOMAS DOUGHERTY

Someone is saying my name
right now, this very minute.
Not *my name* but *my name*
nonetheless, the sound of it.
The same collection of vowels
and consonants that when spoken
make me look. Someone is saying
my name right now to someone else,
whispering it like a lover would,
whispering it in my ear—well,
not my ear, but the ear of whomever
has my name, which I guess
he would argue is HIS name.
And I wonder does he like his name,
and what does it mean to him?
I typed in my name on Internet Search:
3, 336,447 hits.
Who are all these people?
And what do we share, if anything?
Who do those sounds strung together signify?
And the stories behind our name?
What if your last name is Limbaugh?
you might not want to name your kid
Rush, right? There are obvious
ramifications. But Dougherty? Sean"
Put them together and who the hell is that?
How about some guy with a bald head
at a gas station in Utica, New York—
who hears his name over his shoulder,
and turns to see an old high school chum?
That could be happening right now.
It's happened to me. Once, I even got a call

asking for Sean. *Yeah?* Sean Dougherty? *Yeah?*
Sean Thomas Dougherty?   *Yeah what!?!?!*
And they wouldn't believe it was me,
because they were looking for him,
with the slightly deeper voice.
And turns out there was another kid
across town with the exact same name.
People told me he was nothing like me—
whatever that meant. A good student?
For some reason we never met,
never found each other at a party,
or playing ball, which was strange
for such a small city like Manchester,
New Hampshire… Visiting my folks
last winter I ran into an ex-girlfriend
at The Mall who almost fainted.
She said she'd heard I'd killed myself.
I found out later that other Sean
had hung himself in his parent's garage.
What sadness drove that boy?
What loneliness so profound I can't even guess?
And what did whomever found him say?
That name—my name—escaping in a way
I'll never hear from a stranger's lips.
At the wake, friends and relatives must have gathered
to remember what his name meant.
What would I have felt had I been there
to bow my head and listen?
Is that the voice I hear tonight?
Is one of them saying a prayer for him?

COUGH (FOR RUSSELL BANKS)

The snowplow's distant hum is work
That wakes my ears to hear the gangs of school
Children shouting *duck*, snowballs slamming cars—the
    work
Of getting out of bed is next, the work
Of waking my sleepy son—get the paper
From the icy walk, arms out for balance, to scan for
    work
In the classifieds. The worst work
Is *not working*—regretting even the dust
I'd cough hauling bundles at the plant, the dust
That smothers the creases of skin, work
Of loading trucks. A kid leans over to cough
Before getting onto the bus for school, a cough

Against the dust, the wards where coughing
Gnaws the night, where men bend— dust worked
Into the lungs—the doctor touches the chest, cough
The doctor commands. In the novel I'm reading a bus is
    a cough
In a lake—ice breaks, water streams into the school
Bus windows, the children cough
For air, I imagine a reporter caught as he coughs
Into the camera. In this novel
I read about the bus, *someone will make a movie of this,*
    paper
Work is in process—I imagine the writer's cough
In the first meeting, he's hearing the dust
In the pores of his skin, he's hearing the dust

In the hair of his ears, the voices of dust
Have been calling him, he's sees their mouths cough
In his dreams, he sees their eyes, the dust
Is covering his hands, he sees a child breathing dust
Begin to cough. The writer thinks he's upset about the

work
On the script, he cannot sleep, he cannot see the dust
Is entering his lips, he wakes & wipes his face, *dust*
He whispers, *dust of everything. Dust to dust.* The
    school
Where the accident happened is following me, the school
Is visited by reporters, insurance agents, lawyers, dust
Begins to drift in the hallways, people's skin turns to
    paper
With the names of the children written in red ink—paper

Contracts that mean paper money—*where is the paper*
That says forget, the paper that knows it will turn to dust
Before the mothers unfold their hands. In the newspaper
I see the name of the movie, years have passed, the paper
Says *The Sweet Hereafter*—I rent the movie, a cough
Against the dust, the small Canadian town where the
    paper
Ran the names of the drowned—*in the Syracuse paper*
Last week a child is smothered in an ice box, the work
Is what we name it, *the children are sinking under the*
    work
We do not name, the children are fading into *The Sweet*
    Hereafter—paper
Dolls are being cut, they are being strung in the school
My son goes to, I saw them in the hall—*for what?* The
    school

Was filled with the voice of their fragile forms, the
    school
My son rides the bus to, where the teacher knows his
    name. He cuts paper
Into the shape of children *for decoration,* they do not
    talk at this school
What those shapes *mean,* they are "linked hands" the
    school
Does not discuss. The children run in sneakers through
    the dust

Of the yard, they are paper cutouts, silhouettes—school
Is a place of numbers, stickers, stars on papers, first to
        last, school
Is the place where your name is placed on a list, cough
At the wrong time & you will be sent somewhere,
        cough
The doctor said to my son, my son reached
        down—school
Is the place where my son does not want to go, the work
Is getting to him—not the school work, but the work

Of knowing he has been listed, of knowing what is work
That tells *you are only this or that*—what is school
But a place to be told what you are, the place where
        paper
Becomes a series of marks that chart your worth—I tell
        him *it's dust*
That we are made of—when it gets rough, I tell him,
        cough.

THE CHOREOGRAPHY OF 6TH STREET

Tonight the evening wears an Indonesian accent—see the women with their long saris transforming the air into a peacock's tail. Runners sail past raising many colored feathers.   Lithe bodies cutting the wind with their limbs made of movable marble.   I think of Gitanjala "Where the world has not been broken into fragments by narrow domestic walls"—the red bricks of row homes dusting themselves into transparent paper where the children will write their names.   There are bangles from Bali on the arms of the woman raising her laughing daughter.   When the child opens her mouth, O's the color of mangoes float to land like necklaces around my larynx. The little boy with the bandaided knees is bicycling with a blue popsicle—his braided sister pirouettes through the landlord's sprinkler. Behind a screen door, chicken and rosemary do their little dance through the ballroom of the kitchen wind.   The tongue is tasting the air made of many languages. A large woman, pale as the birch tree in front of the boarded church, is singing a hallelujah under her breath.   She wants to rise in the sky and become a cloud, let the rain fall in a baptism of amens.   A boy on his stone steps is eating an enchilada.   His mother, in a red dress and ear-rings from China.   Spanish is changing my ears into green hands/ *Verde te quiero verde.* Let it fall over the coming night.   I look at my shoes, waiting for the bus.   Someone else is here: My right hand is holding his change.   The boy who works at the pizza shop, who slicks back his black hair, under his smock is a shawl of sequins.   There is a gentleness in the way the air holds his head.   Hear the hallelujahs rising from inside us.   Let the air hymn us into remembrance: the sun has almost slipped like a coin in a penny arcade.   This jumbly world.   Gumballs for a quarter.   A gang of small boys sits chewing, blowing bubbles: red, green, yellow, blue.   A Manx cat—a small leopard—sits on the sidewalk yawning.   Everyone suddenly pauses as the sky fills with enormous balloons. The festival is over, the pilots heading south to land their precarious baskets in a field of carnival and clover.   A boy—inspired—stands blowing a bubble the size of his head.   Some of us say he disappeared high into the air that night, carried on the wind inside us. Some of us say he fell back to the curb, to grow toward the sky of pretend.

THE DAY SHAHID DIED

White orchids on the table, curried lamb,
echoes the hands of the tongue. You touch my wrist
like a kiss. The room is green with the scent of papayas,
mangoes, mixed with peppers, eggplants, saffron rice
you swallow, swear to heaven. Your mouth
leans toward my lips. Your perfumed ear,
a thimble of jasmine water, a whiff
of night-soaked lemon trees, you break pan
with two fingers, your gold ear-rings glint.
Your foot brushes my calf, breath of rain
in your sudden kiss. I listen as you lisp
your last letters, Indian beer guzzled.

We stumble into the night, speaking of ghazals,
Shahid'
s sacred songs. As if his lines are incense
one inhales. Kashmir's sitars, broken strings
weeping outside his mother's room. But whose voice
is a violin? Can stroke a cello? Chime the xylophone
of the spine? You ride the train, a man in brown suit snores
so strong it rumbles baritone. His black bowler hat is trimmed
with smoke and blues. Corn bread and hot sauce,
catfish stew. Your fennel breath tastes black as licorice.
Sway to the bassline, lean into the clave of the rails.
I glance at departing strangers. You watch the stations
pass us by. Your close your lids to witness a Gypsy woman

unpeeling a blood orange, petals of peel on her lap. No,
that was years ago. The patter of December rain in Rome.
That pensione was painted gray as ghosts.
She stood outside the train station: her red dress,
her bangles, spray of orange from her hands.
Those children running in the square:
street shrine angels all of them.
Groves of lemon trees. Women tossing green scarves.

Statues that open their eyes. They try to touch your hands.
Paris in the spring: the yellow light that covers everything.
The junkies on the steps of Mountparnasse chew on Pez.
All that was years ago. You open your eyes to eat bread,

brie with black coffee. Unsalted butter on a garlic bagel.
Your eyes are full of elegies. White sails unfurling in your hands.
Those years in Syracuse, the bitter taste of being poor.
Outside of North Side bakeries, counting up change for pastries
Leaning against the brick walls of nightclub alleyways
to hear the bassline drum. Your tongue tasted cheap rum.
You'd hand me a slice of lemon. *Rub it on my breasts,*
bite me lightly with your teeth, you'd tell—bruises bright as plums
bloomed across our skins. I'd braid your golden hair.

Touching my check those nights on buses, trains,
strangers trying not to die. Your mouth tastes of autumn rain.
To roll on quiet rails, our entwined bodies hum:
two guitars that strum Lorca's last casida.
To witness Shahid read was like watching him weave scarves from air.
His words heal the hollow spaces. The hollow hunger of the earth.
Your tongue utters his grace. Your fingers brush my lips.
Your fingers bless my ribs. Our neighbor plays his violin.
Against all walls, Shahid's Sapphics weave the wind.
The blues of strangers' bodies sway on trains of sleep.
In neon'd streets, I ran. The hot dog vendor steams
sauerkraut into the breeze. Fried rice on a fire-escape,

the air of the avenue washed clean after it was rained.
Across how many tables you've reached to hold my face?
I lean into your hands. Your mouth, it tastes of elegies.
How many orchids should we wear? Witnesses for the dead,
we chew in silence. We chew our bread.

THE VIOLINIST'S WIDOW

The suffering that comes with wide shoulders. The suffering that comes in the language of never speaks. The suffering of forgetting being touched by another. The suffering of meanings: when they die we are cut off from ourselves. This suffering. Weary we are sad. Like an important sentence. Like the suffering no one can enter. Absent mindedly. For the book is already old.

This suffering I say. This. For in the morning she dresses. Among the sadness of his not being.

When she lifts her eyes. Like milk. This approaching silence.

And then she hears him, his weeping bow,

AHKMATOVA

In the courtyard, Lorca and Rumi
arguing again over who is more

ecstatic, when Ahkmatova
descends from the shadow forest.

She is wearing a thick, black cape.
Her face is framed with flowers

as if from a funeral. She says,
I am searching for my son.

On her bare throat hangs
a heavy necklace of Russian icons.

She reaches out her open palm,
and there is a tiny photo.

Lorca runs a finger
along the brittle sepia'd boy.

He raises his arms to the sky,
This is the color of Judea.

This is the face
of the brown Christ of Spain.

In the distance guitars
let go their saetas.

Rum is spinning inside of himself.
Ahkmatova, forgive us, begs Lorca,

But she has already vanished.

JEFF GRIENEISEN

CENTRALIA

At the turn of the century,
miners stripped away pines, oaks, and earth,
loaded coal into train cars
for Philadelphia/Reading or Lehigh Valley.
Millions of square tons of anthracite
later, Centralians buried diapers,
table scraps, old mail, broken shoes
next to the vein.
Trapped methane bulged and gurgled
until the abandoned coal seam
whiffed and snuffed with a heat
too intense to be contained.

Smoke still creeps
From the dusty cracked ground,
buckling highways, swallowing homes,
and melting the rubber soles of sneakers
on Ashland teenagers who sneak
into Centralia woods with stolen beer kegs,
their dreams of escaping hidden
like the parched condoms in their wallets.

ECHOES

The river's fluted music hushes.
I descend the hill into the cavern
on the land of the Susquehannocks.

After the harvest, Conestoga men returned
from a hunt or silent war
to lie beside their wives,
women weary of pulling corn.

Enemy of the Five Nations,
this secret tribe canoed the Swatara,
stopping only to carve history
into granite outcrops,
bringing tan skin, pelts, and a tradition
of community.

Not the Iroquois but smallpox
and the Paxton boys left them
extinct.

Now I kneel to study arrowheads,
and I thirst for the water
pooled deep in the cavern's darkness
where they thought the devil himself lived.

LEGACY

We cannot open the box
with her tureen from the old country
for she died too quickly
and it was boxed too carefully.
But we know the story:

On the long boat ride
between the ball that's always being kicked
and Ellis Island, the island of hope,
where she didn't drop
her vowels to fit in,
she clutched only this ceramic weight we know
is emblazoned in Arabian-Spanish
organic design, from Caltagirone.

She ladled fish soup or groundhog stew
into mismatched bowls in the thirties,
a miner's family dinner in Wishaw, Pennsylvania.

After "The Big One," she put it away
to make gnocchi from scratch.
Spaghetti didn't fit, and smelts
needed to lay flat.

After the funeral, her granddaughter, my wife,
lifted only this duct-taped hat box
from the labyrinth of canning jars
and empty jewelry boxes on the floor
of the apartment still spiced with anise and oregano.

DANCE OF THE ANOLES

They spin, face to face,
tails a compass needle never finding home.
They live by the same invisible love
that drives the compass.

Maybe they don't know why they dance--
cocking their little dinosaur heads
up-down-up-down-up. They release
the fiery throat flap as a warning.

When the blacksnake appears,
as he does magically, they will both be gone.
Quiet as water, he swims through the grass,
eats lizards until he's full, then lies in the sun,
and the dance ceases for a while.

MALCOLM'S PIANO

Even as Malcolm no longer remembers
his wife, daughter, or birthday,
he plays piano.
When he used to walk with his wife
through the field
to gaze down the rocky cliff into the sea,
he caught field mice among the swaying weeds,
scratched their ears,
then turned them loose.
Now his eyes no longer focus,
and he draws further away from the window
overlooking the field, further into a place only he sees.
But sit him at a piano and he stops
clasping and unclasping his hands.
His fingers find their way
to the soft sequence he can't otherwise manage—
the melody easier than the words
he can no longer find.

Maybe that's why I play guitar:
so when I'm losing control,
when I forget my wife or my children or how to eat,
my fingers will wrap themselves
around the frets and remember
distant chords I can play
before my family decides
where I should die.
As I slip away from myself,
babbling and slapping at nurses
while they watch me descend,
I can play one last familiar tune.

ORGAN DONOR

To achieve immortality
 Ancient Egyptians required
    the body be intact.
All must be gathered,
entombed together
for afterlife
  inspection.

Death is an accident
    waiting
        to take from us
working parts
    that can be lifted out
                        by careful, quick hands
and planted
        like moist lilies
    into new bodies.

Life brought back in
  the new
body matures into
                two souls, one
                trapped,
the other alive. Does the old soul
        remember? Does
it cry out silently
        inside, wait
        for an exhalation
        to rejoin
the missing frac-
tion that, like Osiris,
            wanders outside
the gate? Does it
        look
with borrowed corneas

for a
liver, kidney, or heart?
Could they be bartered
outside The Gates
when the borrower finally fails?

Skin blushes
pink
from ash-blue death,
or yellow infection.
Blood swells
the new organ with the breath of a new owner
who will spend the rest of his life
rejecting it.

"Every day is a gift"
and the gift of
this meat-colored organ,
this soul-particle,
swims
in the wet cavity
of a new body,
tries to escape,
to find its way back
home,
now buried or burned
to ashes.

WILLIAM HEYEN

WHEELS

The car lot's viper sucked up
stuff from my air that fucks up
atmospheric ozone that blocks rays
that cause cancer & mutate crops,

so okey-dokey & adios to old Rattletrap
who'd lugged my ass ten years of miles
during which I sometimes often glanced
into my rear-view to imagine

ancient jungle translated into gasses
that trapped the planet's heat as in
the glassfront showroom where I dickered
with Flimflam for another set of wheels,

another mirror. With half my mind I wondered
where it was I'd driven, or where be driving
trying to have some fun & make a living....
Hey, my kids will pay it off in time,

the whole package, sunroof & tinted windshield
& a safety airbag guaranteed to fill,
as my life accelerates to open & to close,
with essence of lily & pterodactyl rose.

THE SHOPPER

For as long as they last,
steaks of blue whale calf,
&, marked up by half,
filet of condor's breast,

but when I ate the dodo,
I could not ingest
its gentleness & trust.
Genes lost voyages ago

sometimes seem to snag
in my human heart,
eidolons of Easters past,
but passenger pigeons' eggs

wink in a vanished series,
& the ivory bill cries
in the vacuum of its skies
not at all. Memories

of disincarnate creatures
toll along these aisles,
a great auk smiles
darkly in its freezer

in my human skull,
& my cart follows yours
to checkout counters
cast before us like a spell....

Teach me, Lord,
the evolved wisdom of species
returned to dens & aeries
where all Your mystical dead

still dwell. I cannot find
my daily bread for sale
in this beribboned mall
thronged with the polymer sound

of generic birds on plastic limbs
in plastic trees. I need
to fathom what I'll need
to buy. It's almost closing time

for animals in children's crafts
& artwork on display.
Ruby frogs gray
in anaconda forests

in endangered rain. Before long,
only mutant insects will hover
over the human undersong
because, despite, unless, therefore

this mess of dugong tongue
& memorial prayer,
as the last shopper
clears his choke to sing.

RESPECTS

Junie June-Bug's running joke was "Where's my quarter,
    you better give me my quarter."

Junie, 12, runt of the 6th grade, School 109, Queens—in your face,
    pest & joker, "Where's my quarter,

give me my quarter."... This morning, police arrested Brian Wright,
    16—Brian, called a "Herb,"

a dork or nerd, by others in the hood, couldn't stomach being
    picked on & pushed around,

& this time, when Junie jived him, he pulled a gun from his jacket:
    "You ready to die?" he asked....

Junie turned, took off too late, Brian fired, missed, fired again,
    caught Junie in the back,

fired again. Junie fell to pavement, hard. Brian stood over him,
    shot him again, again,

because, he said, the 6th grader hadn't shown him "proper respects,"
    had "dissed" him....

Minutes later, from her block of shade trees & swept walks,
    Junie's mother arrived on the scene—

"Oh God, my son," she cried, "Hold on, Junior, don't leave me,"
    but the ambulance bore him away,

did not power its siren or red light, & Wanda Carter knew
    her son was dead....

Today, the spot where Junie died becomes a temporary shrine—
    flowers & votive candles where

friends stand in that fusion of grief & joy we humans experience
        when violence ruins or ends

somebody else's life. In any case, the Queens DA tells a reporter,
        "It was a mindless, senseless killing—

"Two kids lost, one dead and one in prison." A neighbor says,
        "Somebody made that gun, somebody

sold it to Brian, our boys are killed for nothing, we've got to get
        weapons off the street."...

Where are we? East of the Apple, now, from that shrine,
        Junie June-Bug scents our minds,

temporarily—"Where's my quarter, where's my quarter, you better
        give me my quarter."

At least, according to police, unlike many other young killers,
        Brian does feel some remorse.

BEAUTY

She told me that during the Second World War
she'd found herself on a Pacific island.
One hot morning, walking forest patched out
by bombs and Seabee dozers, she came upon
the corpse of an enemy soldier. Apparently,

some days before, after a near concussion,
he'd crawled from his hole, and died there.
Now, she tasted a fruit-sweet putrescence in summer air....
But what she needed to tell me, what needed her
to tell this story, what happened to her

was that the maggots swilling in the soldier's face
were golden, a beautiful browngold glistening.
When she saw them, her heart unclenched.
She knew, despite everything she'd witnessed,
she could, possibly, be happy again.

BLACKBIRD SPRING

Mid-morning, walking ocean shoreline,
I found a hundred blackbirds
frozen in ice,
only their heads protruding,
black eyes open,
gleaming, most of their sharp beaks still
scissoring in mid-whistle.

Feeding, they'd been caught
in sea-spray, must be—
all males, up north early,
scarlet epaulettes aflame
a few inches under. I chipped
one bird loose with a stone,
held it in gloved hands

under the rising sun until,
until I realized, until I realized
nothing I hadn't known.
The tide retreated & would return.
Within the austere territories
these would have filled with belligerence
& song, spring had begun.

CYNTHIA HOGUE

THE NEVER WIFE

Eventually, she composed herself,
shards of words, scraps of vellum,
runes to signify at least three directions
sprouting, scrawling. She wrote,
"Nothing, nothing left . . ."

Who was she but a never-wife?
"Feeling around for something lost," inscribing,
now inscribing, "vanished a waterfall
once veiled in mist." Calling her
beautiful, he left; missed her response.

The celebrated 1899 Swedish-Norwegian
race to the North Pole in hot-air balloons
was lost by the Swedes, who vanished
for 43 years, discovered by a US
military survey team, solving the mystery

after they'd been forgotten by everyone
save those who loved and survived them,
their frost-burned bodies half-eaten.
Capt. Erickson's journal detailed the last weeks,
confessing the error of sewing huge sheets

of tarp without caulking (Erickson's
terrible mistake): the balloon seeped,
the team's efforts to keep it aloft failed,
their trek back prevented by an ice floe
(they floated away overnight);

their food ran out. Bjornsson raved for his wife.
Fredickson, trying to fish, was attacked by a bear,

also trapped on the floe. When the last of them,
Erickson himself (taking poison), who wrote
until death, expired, the bear came back.

She died an old woman who, as a young beauty,
was known for her betrothal to Haldor Erickson,
explorer, an historical footnote as compelling
as the victorious Norwegians, because stubbornly
he used uncaulked twine to secure his balloon's seams.

We know her name from a small
country churchyard: *FOSS,*
Anna. And we know what it means:
Swedish for waterfall,
Hebrew for Grace.

MOVING TO NEW ORLEANS

I drive into an August tropic rain.
The road's behind a waterfall and I'm
hunched squinting like a crone
for signs. Ghosts mark the time

I saw there were houses falling down.
The phone had said a 150-year
old Creole cottage in the heart of town.
The corner family as no furniture.

There must be 20 in the place at least.
They speak an English incomprehensible
to me. Their water's shut off last
of every month. They bring me tubs to fill.

I smile, then see *me* in their eyes. The mother
(smiling too) asks, "You David Duke's sister?"

CURTIS

In the rear view mirror,
broad smile; I park when
he walks by. He backtracks

once I'm out: *Do you car*
need washed? lawn? Been
workin' all day, just' $6 more

for rent I got 2 kids
they ma left me with
Anyone ask I tell them all

'bout Curtis Mayhew
I won't lie
I been inside for

armed robbery I was very
nervous I'm fine
now doin' right

jus' the landlord
won't wait   kids don't
eat but I put a roof

over they heads one
room I'm not wild I'm
tryin' hard for the kids

There's a moment our eyes meet
before I stop believing
the bone-thin man before me

who has no children, no room—
who will come back each week
now that I go inside

for the six dollars to hand him
off the porch, like a penance
for living on White Street.

MOVING TO WHITE STREET

Mr. Fautaux takes in the morning sun,
asks how old I think he is. Lying
by 20 years, I say 65. Now,

he waits with secrets of his youthfulness—
brewer's yeast, milk, and garlic.
His wife liked her beer too well

and being a *hard-headed woman*,
died of drink long ago. His girlfriend
liked to kiss, but she had a bad heart

and garlic gave her gas so she wouldn't
take it and died too. Garlic
does not give Mr. Fautaux,

reeking around the corner, gas.
He brings me the column
on quitting smoking by Dr. God.

Says real estate men like to talk
(trapped again, I believe him), and
fingers a ramshackle house

moved off Esplanade before his time
by a famous Basin Street whore
when she got too old. *Wanna know*

how to make a fast sale? Find
a house in a white neighborhood,
go door to door saying:

"You never know who will buy.
In a few days, the place sold.
Worked every time."

He smiles and waves
at his black neighbors,
who smile and wave back.

Do you like to kiss?
I like to kiss.
You wouldn't want to kiss

one of them, would you?
Why not come up on my porch,
and stop awhile?

CROSSING CRESCENT CITY CONNECTION

(Ed's Story)

Last fall I moved across the river
and sometimes to watch the lights
would walk home over the bridge.
It was so misty that night
you couldn't see the city or—
I don't know why I walked—
the water for the dark.

It was like walking over nothing
into nothing though I didn't think this
at the time, but of my young son, another soon,
and what I want to give them in life.
Also of my wife. He was so still
I wouldn't have seen him, but he coughed.
He sat out where a girder joined an arch.

What you doing man? I called,
feeling dumb. What *could* one say?
Whatever comes; I later understood
how circumstance leaps away from words.
I was surprised he answered, not what
he said but that voice over the river:
Nobody care if I live or die.

I said, *Come home with me, brother.*
He didn't move one way or the other
so I thought, He's listening.
Come to my house for dinner, man,
then if you still feel no one cares
I'll walk you back to this bridge,
and push you off myself.

Soon the police arrived, pushing me aside
as they crawled toward him. He cried,

Leave me alone, and, *You make another move*
I'll jump. As if they'd heard those words
a thousand times but never meant,
they came on. He stood up.

I saw how thin he was, and helpless,
watched him with deliberation—
the next-to-last act of his life—
push up his sleeves before he dove,
silent, into a larger silence
where we could not follow,

falling without ourselves, but left
with ourselves, men on a bridge
thinking (without thinking)
as we turned toward home
we might have girded
the girderless air.

WHAT MATTERS TODAY IS THE
SPIRIT OF THE MODERN

When scientists claim truth
it hurts them more than
hermeticism (which sparkles).
Bawdy and vulgar, they'll look a tree in the eye
and spit nails: "I shall die pig-drunk
if you don't save me."
But don't.
          Bitter
memories refresh the moment.
Emptiness becomes us until
our senses are dispossessed by the extraordinary
and "we must jouk and let the jaw gang by."
Acknowledging the inclusion of all experience,
we think nature bestows
consolation, something richer than habit,
like old valleys of continuous
flow and cultural pieties.
Far form the totalitarian,
one's body "passes authorities,
false bowing to landlords
of dissemblance."
               In the 12th century
pilgrims readied for each season
as if the world meant to cease
its revelations, stuttering,
breathless. "Old spirits like new
woke to bells in the village,
ringing. Silvery, the rosy day."
One was asked, *Didn't you wake up*
when they broke in? and said,
No, I didn't wake up yet now see
"the earth is not a building
but a body depending upon
supreme mutability and power to change

the Rule of Things clearly":
a truth inscribed on parchment weathered
beyond recognition by the elements,
                    "the ear following
                    the stars' path" for one
                    miraculous instant.

HENRY HUGHES

CALLING DOWN THE GEESE

He's calling down the geese,
my uncle, low in the gray hull.
His face billows with blowing
through a wooden throat
a note all December, all bird.
He's blind. Once a savage—
beating his wife on Christmas.
I know that, watching him
listen downwind. He smiles, suddenly,
holding my arm to be still. *Be still.*
I forgive. I love this moment.
He's calling down the geese,
the gander's ear, its memory,
breath drawn across the bony reeds.

EATING WHALE

Niigata, Japan

Whale, there,
right in the supermarket.
So I make a soup. To taste crime
is to believe in yourself.

I close my eyes like God,
thinking feet gone to flukes,
my fabulous tail. Seagrass, turtles,
steely blue fish—
all this
and the fatty sound
between my teeth
crackling like a billion bubbles.

IN THE DOGHOUSE

Once loved,
there's the eternal quilted hill above the floor.
No mosquitoes, no rain. Your antless dish
in the kitchen. And she strokes you,
rubs your ears. Until you slip-up—
chew the table leg, hump the wrong guest,
eat a cheesecake,
pee.

You're in the dog house,
on that rusty chain of words bolted to a stud.
There's a leafy wind, cat prints
pucker the sandy plywood floor.
You're alone. It's damp. Greasy fur pinched on a nailhead.
Sniff the corner, turn
and drop. You're not sorry,
you do your time.

TOGETHER IN THE ICE-STORM

I'd pour burning vodka over the trees
if it would help
melt that killing weight. The thought works
for a while, until sadness extinguishes
anger's blue flames
and your hair drops long
into the white basin.
I'm sorry, I say, touching your back.
But you can't hear below those creamy falls,
roots slipping from tunnels of autumn's love
before the right breast sunk, before the chemo
and the Pacific sky
surprising with combination trouble—
a little harmless snow, then freezing rain, then cold cold.
Even the evolved go down like dinosaurs
in an ice-storm.

Smoking a cigarette on the porch,
I hear the gunshot crack of a limb
that might save a groaning maple.
If only we'd make it to the sun—
crystal pains letting go
and shattering to earth
like windows of a cruel church.
Back inside for another drink, I see clippers
and a towel, your bald crown in firelight.
You're beautiful, I say, so close to truth,
it catches and burns.

STEELHEAD ALMOST

Too dark to retie,
they walk fishless over the bridge,
break-down rods and unboot
for the dry drive home.
Oh well, one man says. *That's fishing.*
The other doesn't want to talk. There's a barbecue tomorrow.
If you catch something, she said. *That'd be wonderful.*

Following headlights, he feels again
                    that strike behind the stone—
cherry-blushed chrome, leapsilver and dive.
Then gone. Canyon pouring river,
swallows spading air. The trees shrug
as if nothing happened.

In a hole deeper than sleep,
the steelhead
                    undulates fragrance and flow,
                              nudging forward—
three thousand orangey eggs
in her bright sleeve.

JEFF KNORR

MOTHER'S COOKING

I expected to see her over a pot of soup,
a spattering pan of meat, steak and onions,
or her long arms dressed white in flour.
Long before we'd parted on the porch,
she'd given me the warning to stay
away from the creek, all it's deep suck holes
and drifters hanging around the banks mysterious,
invisible as wind—instead we feared ourselves.
And, funny, but she never warned us about the fences
we climbed, the utility workers we dodged, dissolving
like clouds into the bushes, and what about the spillway
we fished directly beneath—all of this a secret.
I wanted to show her the cardinal I found
as dead and orange as the one from her girlhood.
The day we found the deer skeleton in the shallows,
the pearl-white bones searching for the current,
was the same day I left three bright rainbow trout
to die on the bank, for birds to peck meat off thin curved ribs
that would not to be dredged in flour, fried in butter and parsley.
Pedaling home in the hot summer afternoon, I knew
the hamburger we'd eat for dinner would hold the secret
of fish in its sweet, dripping fat, that I'd go back for years
to that deer and stare, looking for the right way of the water.

GOOSE HUNT, JUST BEFORE CHRISTMAS

Walking the length of the apple orchard under a long blue sky
we might think it is a day when December has forgotten itself.
But frost on the apples tells us otherwise.
And quail in the brush alongside the creek stay down then run
along the draw, their scents hanging for the dog like tiny shadows.
We have come this far and what we know is little.
It will be a day of friends, of some proportionate eating,
a little bit of whiskey, conversation, then long bouts of silence.
We will watch ten thousand geese come in low, each of them
just skirting the weight of our small necessities.
And soon this week the dead and dying will sit at our tables
and we will honor them for what they might show us.
What we know is that we have already come this far.
The sun beats against us and we break ice around our legs.
Setting decoys in the pond, our feet slip on the slick bottom
which will be dry and cracked like an Arizona wash by late July.
And I go to recounting: days when pheasant rose a week before the season,
gunning quail out of the old farmhouse on the White River,
watching the moon set through cottonwoods on Grand Island,
a meal of gumbo and braised duck and zinfandel.
And the breeze against my neck startles me with cold. The numbing hands
turn my mind in the quick shift like glassy eyes of spooked chukar.
And I wonder what this trembling afternoon will hold for us,
pointing blue steel toward the sky, shooting into the peace over grassfields
that holds birds steady until one of them is lost and the others circle.
Now that we have come this far we cannot retrace our steps
through the orchard or follow the scent of birds who have fled.
This will only lead us to an invisible place. We will break rows and
rows of frozen apples dripping in this cool December afternoon
hoping with the certainty of dusk to find the edge of the orchard.

MONTANA ELK

For Jan Warner

Today the elk have moved far up Mack's Canyon.
They herd in a stand of fir and aspen,
snow settling on their thick brown shoulders.
Antlers become the low limbs of trees.
Their hot breath steams from nostrils, disappears
into the gray wet sky that has come to touch them.

This day you must be with them. I imagine
in the cold, blue morning the crack of the Remington
rolled from the back porch around the canyon,
your final shot, the muzzle just behind your chin
flying into the sky like magpies.
And you lifted out of an unfamiliar body
its sagging skin, tired feet, the cancerous stomach.

This day I'd like to think you're with the dead mother
of your boys, the glow of the thick-pitch warming
fire snapping from a tired stump.
And one evening in November when the light
falls toward purple in the gathering cold
your sons will be working two sides of the draw
in knee-deep snow, each with one of your guns.
As the bull breaks loose from the bottom,
you might speak into each of their ears.
In the surprise, you stop their shots, the elk
dissolves into the trees, your voice lost in the wind,
reminding them this day they'll remember
the twilight moon coming from the east,
flakes breaking out of the clouds, the yellow fire
up the draw, their own hot breath in the dark cold.

WALKING BEFORE BREAKFAST

To wake me, the dog has nosed my right foot three times.
The toes point like a fir tree under the wool blanket,
and I'm ready to kick her at the next pass.
Instead I rise, to the cold, a few bright embers
banked in the fire still wheezing out heat.
The night has pulled its black cheek
from the windows and is leaving.
The outline of birch trees will set the sky burning
yellow in one hour. They might take me
walking sooner than I have the past week
but the panting at my side needs one biscuit,
and the woman who has trapped my heart
with her eyes for the last fourteen years
needs a fire snapping by seven.
The dog chutes like a bull by the back door.
Two doves startle from beneath the myrtle.
Later, walking, I will just crest the ridge
find my dead grandfather whittling under an oak,
then a young boy in the rustle
of crisp manzanita leaves just off the trail.
I will bring my son home a piece of quartz
white like snow that has decided to remain all year.
At the end of the path is Spicer Lake
and the wood duck. We have seen each other before.
But on this morning we are closer than usual and still.
She must think I look foolish with this rock, my pink
skin, worms of veins on the backs of my hands.
We watch until I spook her with an uncontrollable
twitch of my left fingers. Slapping the water,
wings dip the surface, she rises
and is gone, a spot cresting the far trees.
She has taken a piece of me
I will never find again. If I'm lucky
she'll set me in the reeds in an Oregon lake
so I might wash ashore at the feet of a fisherman.

Coming home, the fire blazes, the house creaks
its old timbers. Breakfast steams on the table.
If there is any finding ourselves again
let it be in the throats of birds, the cup of light
reflected in a pool, the eyes of a different man,
the moment each day cracks open like a stone.

BREAKING WATER

Thigh-deep in Gerle Lake, the water is so calm
you'd think nothing but stone was beneath.
But occasionally a water snake slips along shore
and trout surface sucking insects, the slurp
rippling the portrait of forest running across the cove.
Behind my right shoulder is an old grinding rock
and seventy-two miles past that is my hometown
sitting in the valley heat still as the green surrounding me.

On my line, I have knotted a dry fly my dead grandfather tied,
thinking if I slice tight loops of line through the air
its wings will create a song I cannot hear, its tiny barbs of feather
bend back and hum so that only the ghosts might listen.
I cast hoping the fish will come, and after so many
times without thinking, I believe I know where they all are,
where they've been in the darkness of stumps and stones,
the way the fly lands and leaves breaking the water
can deliver spirits, that my grandfather might rise
straight from the rocky bed of this cove.

GERRY LAFEMINA

SERENDIPITY CAFÉ

Returning, we saw the burning, and I'd never seen a building
pregnant with flame before, so we stopped on a stoop one block from the heat
and watched walls melt around the frame, windows diving for the street
while cinders ascended on an escalator of atmosphere.

I'll admit fear, something primordial, traceable, I bet,
to our australopithicus forebears. It was Homo Erectus that learned to leash
the rabid mouth of fire. The inventions that followed: the abacus,
the bow, the phonograph. I listened to the Clash's first album the night
the Serendipity Café blazed and raged, and I regret

not going the next day to witness the barricades and arson pros
sifting the soot, and a group of regulars later searching for a piece
of their lives— their after-work coffee, their toast— in a twist of stool
or a cut of cracked counter-top. At last experts declared kitchen grease

caught alight. It was that quick and easy and I forgot
to mention no one died that night, not a waitress or a busboy
or some young loving couple. No one. That night the cafe earned its name,
while the young waiters stood outside staring and one of them
cupped his hands to light a last cigarette. Only a match. Only its flame.

NIAGARA

In this park I see a deaf couple talking,
their fingers practicing acrobatics in the space
between them, their eyes deciphering
subtle innuendos that time together creates. People walk past
oblivious but for a little boy
who mimics the fluttering digits
and then laughs hard at the movement of his hands.

The echo of that laughter is sacred
for its slim volume of joy. And the signed sweet-nothings
are sacred too. And the rushing water

plummeting from the cliffs: a baptismal.
We know the stories— the brave with their barrels
versus the violence of water: daredevils seeking a cleanliness
only the white explosion of river against rock-and-river
can create.
                The spray painted mist of the falls.

Moisture in my palms.

Were I able I'd wash my hands in the falls, purify
the sins from my fingertips—
this dirt, this earth. My own fallibility.

The young boy's dancing down the path
in front of his parents, or one of his parents
and that person's new love— it's so complicated
this loving.
                I heard
once that a woman loved the Virgin so much
she envisioned Her image in the spray. No surprise.

She may have been my neighbor. She may have lived
alone at the end

        and ate nothing but Saltines.
And spoke to the shadows that appeared
on the walls, addressing each with the name of a saint.
I never knew her,

just saw her frail paper-white and paper-thin hand
reach for the mail each morning;

                          but I recall the evening
squad cars parked in her driveway
and an ambulance. All that speed— too late.

Too late.
        Night encroaches on this park now,
kicks couples one by one from the benches,
some of them summoned to supper,
others to their preternatural passions:
                        water falling.

If I could reach across this river I'd put my hands in the Falls
and cup myself a drink. I can't,
so instead I touch a puddle with my fingers
and bless myself the way I was taught
with the still waters of the ordinary world.

EMPTIES

I still enjoy these nights— a storm forming to the east
and me with a porch seat. I still forget some times
that I don't need to leave at ten for the club
and the inevitable clash with some drunk
whose mouth was louder than the crash

of guitars and bass and cymbals. I still like my music loud,
although some nights I miss the brash pogo stick
of conversation with waitresses and regulars. And after I wheeled out

the trash, after the empties had been stacked
and the cooler filled with Millers, I'd sit with a twelve-ounce, my body unstable
and stuttering on a bar stool as I stared through the picture window,

like a failed clairvoyant. And of two friends I worked with then?
Who knows.

Chris Lee with his ivy of violet braids, the tattoo of a teddy bear
clutching a machine gun on his arm, and his exhibitionist fables,
always another woman; and the other Chris

for whom fear was a racist cop, enjoyed his food and his dope almost
as much as he loved to laugh— a deep eruption
emanating from his bone girders outward to his 280 pound girth.

I still see them some nights, the same way
I'd see their reflections after closing,
standing behind me at the star-fighter game,
and beyond them the bartender vending one last illegal shot to the soundman.
A band breaking down in the distance.

The rain still fills the potholes on Michigan Ave.,
the wet tarmac stretching the stolen light of street lamps the length of a block.
I still like my music loud—
and in bars all over America punk rock kids are plugging Stratocasters
into patchwork amplifiers. It makes me happy

this rain, but it reminds me of big Chris who stripped his shirt
one night and stood in the street singing
what? I couldn't hear. He started soaping himself
with the night. Rain filled his near-empty bottle
and soon he sipped big and frowned as if suddenly he knew

his future and it frightened him. Then he ran off,
his body slick and brilliant with perspiration and rain
so he almost shined like obsidian

while Chris Lee and I stayed by the window, our hair shivering. *Shit,*
he said, not as an expletive but as a defeated act
of vocabulary— his inability to choose a different word.

I still like my music loud. I still like storms like this one,
all the rain close to home, all the lightning
miles away, so there's no thunder, no sounds at all

but for the sanitizing drum roll of the shower
on the roof and the tread of loud, individual drops which strike the soft earth,
setting what it holds free.

PAWN TO KING FOUR, ETC.

With this steaming cup of Sumatra blend
blowing wispy by my side, I watch high school boys playing chess
and think of my father at the Village Chess Shop

paying a quarter to play Bobby Fisher,

a barefoot college kid shambling
around a U of 25 tables, going one by one,
choosing a move and moving on. *Never once*

my father says, *did Fisher make a mistake.*
Never once did he lose.

How many games have I played

with old men from Russia or Italy or the States,
all those accents behind the black-or-white armies,

a veritable UN of accents—

stories of pogroms and occupations
and an occasional chuckle or *check* or *hmph*.

Thus chess is an international language that I once knew fluently,

studied it even in the *Times*, setting up the board
and making each move in a given game: P-K4, etc.

The headlines, read, folded away—
Libya, Lebanon, Iran, Nicaragua. Meanwhile
on the streets barefoot old men warmed themselves by heating grates,
one of them possibly Fisher himself in his paranoia. Saturday

afternoons of protest: placards and chants; evenings of chess or pool;
then the restless chords of punk bands. So many girls

I desired and failed even to talk to.

I knew chess, the news, the simple physics of nine ball and
the frustration of my own insecurities.
In this way I was like the teens here:

the one pushing his glasses back up his nose
before touching his white bishop, deliberative; the one who says
This Iraq business is all about the oil. Nothing else.
I realize now I saw these kids Thursday at the peace rally

downtown; they were cutting class, no doubt with some teacher's
blessing, and I gave them my own too.

That day's headline: **Shock and Awe—**
the proposed 800 cruise missiles to be launched into Baghdad
the first three days. 800 is the number of weeks it's been

since I was 18. 800 is the first three digits of a toll-free call.
Who can I call to complain about the war drums banging?
Would anybody listen? One kid says

this is the president's gambit and exhales loudly.
I'm looking for Bobby Fisher, the next great American
hope. I'm looking for
one chance to beat my father at chess. He tells me

he never lasted more than 16 moves against Fisher
except one day he went 31.
                              This seemed like a victory.

One kid says he's heard talk of reinstating the draft
and he's scared.
                    Silence like a small flock of sparrows descends

until the kid who could be me says check;
his opponent goes *hmph*. One of them mentions Renee and remarks
how beautiful he thinks she is

and their off detailing her outfit or her hair

or comparing her to other girls in Trigonometry.
I know none of these names. I know them all.
The woman I call beautiful is miles away. Bless her

and those boys, their lust and fear. Their longing. Bless
the girls they name and their basic shyness.
Bless Bobby Fisher, wherever he is, and my father.

Bless his absence too

and the young men in Baghdad moving chessmen in a café
discussing girls they think are lovely,

bless them also and protect them in their beautiful ruined city
which, when I close my eyes, I fear is already burning.

LINES ABOUT LONGING AND ROOFS

June in the shade of television antennae:
　　a MacDougal Street walk-up,
the roof's tar still tacky with daylight,

their bodies possessed with the fallen
　　angels of rhythm and melody,
which they celebrate, eight stories above asphalt—

the sensual hymn of muscles extending,
　　flexing. Pausing, they watch flies
tango in the dank air of their sweat,

the atmosphere of their flesh
　　damp with dance. Come morning
she wants to see the shower's spray

flamenco on the ballroom of his belly
　　and back. When he steps
from behind the curtain she'll stand ready

as an exorcist, holding a towel
　　stolen from one of the rooms
where they squandered their thousand nights.

MEDITATION ON AN ABANDONED FARMHOUSE

You see them some days, cumbersome husks
in distant fields, their walls sagging under the weight
of years neglected or the nagging memory
of a fire caused by a careless cigarette

or the zig-zag atmospheric match of lightning: old barns
or farmhouses— the window glass now nothing
but dust, and the names of those who once lived
there now only a word the wind mispronounces.

And wandering these woods sometimes
you may happen on the remains of a whole hamlet
that gave up when they discovered the land's
inarable or a plague came or, more likely, they were just

homesick for family nine months behind and were failing
to make a living: the citizens one by one packed some things
back into wagons, hitched the horses
and left the buildings to animals—
                                        rodents and spiders, then owls

moving in until the walls withered and slumped into kitchens.
The wood inevitably rotting. Now only the stones
of hearths, the few crosses
in a cemetery. If you believe the folklore,

one of these grave sites has two death dates
etched into its stone, and now no grass grows
above the plot, and the trees there reaching heavenward
— what should be burly oaks— are only leprous birches.

Every summer weekend local teens go there with cases
of Budweiser to frighten each other with stories
of hexes stolen from horror films, but the only curse

around is the sworn *Goddamn* of a woman in a kitchen,
her family gone on hard times. And driving today past trailer houses
heavy with heating bills, their sidings latticed with doilies of grime
and the cards the wind deals, you can imagine them already abandoned—

the '75 Cutlass on blocks suffering
its dandruff of rust, the Chevy Impala,
hood agape, tires deflating; the living room windows
undressed, and inside, an argument

or the back of a hand against a cheek. You can't hear the weeping.
Just the wind banging a screen door open and closed.
Open and closed. All of it
passes so quickly that if you blink it'll be gone

even should you pull over. And you'll be standing there
at the pavement's edge, your hands pocketed as road dust
irritates your eyes so they sting for awhile
as if you might grieve. Instead you blink three times
turn and walk across a former pasture
into the cool breath of this cruel and beautiful earth.

HARRIET LEVIN

SHE RAN

on a path of golden and crimson leaves, everything falling drifting into her.
Sweetgum. Ginkgo. Her legs ached, her thighs quivering against the raw
weather, breathing in gasps. She ran, her iPod playing Costello, speeding,
speeded up, the way light travels, planets spin and meteors collide leaving
a hole in the earth. She ran, her laces slipping out of their knots trying to
break free of the soft earth a footprint adheres to marking her tread. She
ran, her hair conferring with wind, blocking her face, shielding her eyes, each
turn a wall mixed with some dark and some flashing some brilliant pieces
of mica hauled from a pit to shine here. She ran when the path broke onto
cement, crossing the blacktop to the other side, stalks of bamboo filtering
sunlight. The road is doubtful. The road splits then stops. See, if you rest
if you crouch down even for a moment you will lose the energy to find it
again, such sharp, such intractable edges. She leapt forward, her sneakers
skidding down the curb. In the late afternoon she is not dead like tree limbs
that flicker in the sun besieged with light.

GIRL IN CAP AND GOWN

Next morning
over coffee
on the porch of a guest house
in a seaside town, I'm introduced.
Tom says, "You're the girl in the street
last night we called Kim. The one who looks like Kim."
Bob swallows a sip
then amid the clatter of china says,
"You could be Kim's sister."

I say I don't know who she is
and because it is raining outside,
the yellow tarpaulin over the upstairs deck
flapping in the wind,
filling with emptiness,
I go back to my room.
They're still there
when I come down,
sprawled out on the glider.

They scrutinize me, darken my hair,
square off my chin
and I am blotted out. I cannot hear
my own thoughts, voice, story.
The rain and the slap of waves.
The clatter of china. The flapping tarpaulin.
Until at last I'm off the porch,
having reached the path,
standing in the salvaging downpour
but you have to realize I am writing this
after I have found out.

At the end of that path
I walk smack right into
a pole (literally bumping into it

because it is raining and I walk face down)
where someone stapled a photocopy
onto the gouged out wood
of a girl in cap and gown
splattered with raindrops
staring at me that reads:
KIM MISSING LAST SEEN IN WELLEFLEET
6/22/06

I gasp. So this is Kim.
It doesn't matter anymore who she is
or I am or if we resemble one another
or not at all—it had been a pick up line
or at best a punch,
if Kim were not already dead.

What happens is
they put me in her place
at the bottom of a deep ravine.
I close my eyes. I hold my breath,
the possibility becoming next.
And then it stops,
and I come back.

A LENS

It's as if she can't stop seeing existence
through a lens of rape.
Doesn't she have anything
else to write about, things for instance
that if looked at objectively or if refracted
can bend their properties

change states like water, evaporate and dissolve

endure extreme fluctuations in temperature on a faraway planet,
yet retain their elementary bonds

well enough to demonstrate the eviscerating?

Violence doesn't evolve,

its fists and neck-choking hands do not follow the evolutionary chain,
so don't waste your beautiful imagery describing monsters
who snap like the short end of the wishbone,

never the half that makes the wish.
They rip through tendons—you ought to write
         about someone who greets with more decorum,
leans over a table, learns to balance a water
chestnuts on chopsticks, insulates
layers of Ghirardelli foil to form something distinctive from crown

                                                            to
                                                            rump,

bipedal, feathered—something glorious like a phoenix rising above fire escapes
and rising over the city, blazing with more light and heat
than the jangle of lights below.

She must be doing it
because she wants to be gang banged, fucked like a Yanomami
girl, legs bent so far back

    they refract like water in a glass
among the unreflecting panes of glass
in a house, in an entire neighborhood of glass.

HEMLOCKS

These hemlocks swaying
mock the circle of trees
towering my parent's house,
trees that bear no fruit.

No Macintosh. No Russet.
We forfeit nothing by touching them.
I know nothing more
than what I see looking out through rain,

through the steamy window half-open,
when my mother smiling says,
Imagine the road is the bay.
I don't want to imagine the boardwalk, the sand

the horizon. I want to be there.
These hemlocks separate our house from other
houses, patios, swimming pools, the backs
of parents' heads. Why don't they turn around

and watch us dive into the deepest part
of the water? We emerge shaking,
baring our bodies in the sun.
The hemlocks are a border we can't see beyond

or cross, like the night my father chased us,
when we wouldn't leave our friends, and he tripped
over a branch. In the darkness we laughed,
not one of us rushing to help him inside,

crushing our cigarettes on a curbstone.
Life a succession of images
these hemlocks planted in a row,
green and enduring, we take for the whole.

IBIZA

I wish I could bumble and buzz
transfer honey to the tongue
of the stranger gyrating his hips,
his drink in his hand,
and lick off the salt rim
encrusting his tongue stud

with the unsullied swagger
of honeybee daggers in captivity
for three thousand miles
when their crate doors swing open
on almond blossoms.

When I sashay up, he recognizes me
as if after 18 years, an event more momentous
than the honeybee release, because at that moment
someone bumps my elbow
and my drink spills and his drink spills
and as he reaches over
to help assemble
the ghostly broken vessels

his knuckles brush the crotch on my too tight jeans
I'd like to hurriedly remove.
Is it just the clinging material
or my soul cleaving
or the solely material
weave of airways
collapsing the dark caves
beneath my eyes?

My fingers let go
stinging with ardor
as if into the bower
of each open flower.

BOY SOLDIER

So hard to balance the picture in this morning's
paper of a Congo soldier—age twelve—balancing a rifle
across his chest, his innocence in camouflage,

his eyes so bloodshot they portend rivers
risen high above their joists.
Ignominious rains languor and overlap.

The rains take lilies in their clutch.
They take the innate, negligible blossoms.
The photo borders the box where the day's

winning lottery tickets are posted. The glamour
of the winner drives the spinner.
There's no time to consider the dreary font

of a dredge, and I'm unbalanced, grainy,
paying in splits, flicking ashes, and everything else
I look at this sun-soaked, withering October

day is so set on edge, so ready to tip.
The photographer balances the legs of his tripod
over a rut in the road, the whirls on my fingertips as black

as when the psychic held my hand and read
the break in the line, while the next girl dipped
her finger in lip gloss. I'd like to spread her shine,

dab it on in lodes looking for a way to make amends
with others and with myself. A dusky grouse.
A turkey vulture. Even these

lift up. They fly slantwise. They find a vein
to convey them southerly
and go forth astride this tilted earth.

SCOTT MINAR

THE CHILDREN WHO GOT UP FROM THE HEAP OF CORPSES

They got up, they got up, they got up, they rose, they rise, they half-bloom, death's day flowers, they fell, they fell, they fell, they stumbled, they got up, they got up, they ran, they ran wildly, out of the moment almost, they shook, they shook, they shook in an abyss shaped inexactly like them, they ran, they ran, they ran, what time could make, they got up, they got up, they vaulted, they seized the smallest part of their death day, they asked, they wanted nothing but to be awake in the comfort of some stranger's arms before they died.

THUS I COULD ENJOY THE FULL BENEFITS OF DEMOCRACY ONLY AS A CORPSE

As a corpse I could repeat myself and no one cared. No one waited for me at a station, no visitors asked my address. I got lost in my country and found a way out. My street disappeared, my house was tortured and told everything. I left my shoes scattered like closet leaves. These are the full benefits of corpse-life: no address book, no clothes, no identifying numbers, any room in the basement.

ONE VERSION OF THE STORY

The boy waits inside his adolescence like a stranger riding the train. He is unsure of the stops and everyone is speaking a strange language. A boy waits inside the room of his sex. He is bleeding milkweed. He is lost anger turned to something else, rigid as a board, bird-corpse stiff. Nothing knows the past like a window. A window throws everything back, shuddering in a rainstorm; it reflects like still water. The boy waits inside his past. The rooms fill with wisteria and wildflowers. I can't tell you any more. The train is gone, like the boy.

THE ALLEGORY OF THE MINEFIELD

What blows you apart is not found in the field.
It is in the mind that tendons stretch and break,
kneecaps blown away like a tissue snatched by the
wind. Inside her crutches, the girl has rolled up a
message: I was long and beautiful, a new thing in
this world. Meanwhile on the campus of the war
machine, dark leaves are falling. In the fourth world,
someone walks on the ends of his thighs.

THE ICE-AX

Trotsky's last minutes were struggle: the assassin beaten back in shock like pigeons scattering in the square, taken up by the wind of him. He loosened the weapon from Jacson's hand, bit him as a wasp, and then bleeding like a waterfall refused to collapse on the floor in front of him. His guards roused, his wife running to him, he stood in the doorway and waited, arms limp at his sides like dead eels. The wonder of it all: Natalya holding his face in her hands, and he over and over again returning her kisses.

WE WERE ORDERED TO COLLECT THE CHILDREN, BUT THEY DID NOT APPROACH ME, SO I SAT WATCHING HOW THEY COLLECTED THE CHILDREN

They collected the children like fish in the air but the children were not dead, were not even still but flopping half limp at the belly mostly arms and legs still waving, kicking and palming the dark like blind tigers, such brave gestures impotent as a flower and then there came the time when there were no more children or they all stopped fighting at once or the darkness flopped over my eyes like the canvas door of my last night I can't tell but it all stopped at least for me and I felt the wind through my belly a rocket through my head eyes shot upward in a fierce jerk toward the sunlight though it was hard to turn away from the children.

JERRY MIRSKIN

ICARUS

To understand this story
you have to picture a gate hanging open
and let that gate be the sun.
Then picture a boy bursting from the spell
of too much dark, how he tumbles
and slips from the effortless grip of the clouds.
What seemed last night like a good idea,
spanking the water.
I don't really understand why he had to die
beyond understanding the statute of limitations–
how imagination goes unsupported in the sky.
I suppose I understand how water goes on living,
while people like you and me prophesy a kind of patience
a pride in flying low, a wisdom
in the plain joy of just walking around.
But, to really understand this story
you have to imagine a kind of castle loneliness.
Nights when there is no telling
from all the things that men do, just what we want to do.
From that flightless dark
it is just a small step to seeing any sign of sun
as the kind of beauty our knowing can embrace.
Maybe it is just youthful infatuation,
but who wouldn't open their arms?
Who wouldn't feel in the light of such knowledge
like putting on their wings and going out?
Picture a gate hanging open.
And let that gate be the sun.

ROCK AND WATER

They were a perfect pair.
The boy hunched over near the rocks.
His shadow moving gently on the surface
as if he were stirring the water.
When you looked closer, you could see
that he had something in his hand.
A small silver fish.
He was stroking it. Placing it in the water
in swimming position.
It floated to the surface and lay on its side.
Once, twice.
The sun shone on the side of the fish
and the boy continued.
Nearby another boy stood with a fishing pole
facing the other way.
He was busy and only looked over once in a while.
The boy continued trying to help the fish
by adjusting it in the water, placing it in motion.
Patiently and deliberately, as if placing the last piece
in a puzzle. As if it only needed a little help, a touch.
Once in a while the fish would actually stir on its own
and then it would slip to the surface as if having died again.
Each time the boy seemed more intent
and repeated his stroking, hovering like a guardian
repeating this ritual of patient affection and concern.
It was a very clear day. The water and the light glittered.
I stayed until I couldn't watch any longer.
Hovering as if to understand.
They were a perfect pair.
The little fish did not know how to go on living.
And the boy did not know how to let it go.

CLAMFLAT

A bay without the ebullience of water. Half bog,
half slick bladder. An open room. A ruminant eminence
that pulls on our mudded boots. A stage.
To me, it's all about what will will pile onto a plate in a few hours.
Though for you– I watch as you bend to the task– it's the catch
you'll gather into the livelihood of your "kibbin." A cute name
for a wire basket that airs the cool draught of this uncovered reservoir,
this dank sphere risen from withdrawn water.
Picture a cool plain, above which a collage of grey gulls salt the air
with the misery of their song.
For these paupers it is all wheel and hover.
For them there is no other place.
And when they get like this above the bare bay,
they barely have to work it.
The sleek dog– he don't care– will show us how it's done.
This one lights out over the surface of the smooth world like a mop.
And I wish I could wake like that. Run like centrifugal rhyme
barely touching the round plain of the world.
Muscle being and more.
Nevertheless, he cannot betray the indigenous misery of the bay.
This "Stinkflat," as you say, when the rank and ancient odors
catch the lining of your brain.
That's where the birds come in. Two sticks in the air– the needle
of their beaks on the revolving plain– and Voila!
A few minutes of gyre and it's all aria and epithet.
Or in your case epitaph.
Translate: The body is made to be broken.
You are made to bend with your back to the highway and sky.
How many of us know how cold and wet a man might feel
after hours of digging?
In a few hours, I'll uncurl from the curved handle of the rake,
drag the weak prop of my body to the car–
go home and take a bath.
And with that thought another comes from the semaphore
of tired limbs: Maybe she'll be there. Maybe she'll open the door.

The real question is, when one finally stands after bending
to the earth's cold mire, will one say that all one wants to be
in this world is a man?
You stand, and for a moment I can see your mind revolve.
The air, a rank below sea level, is bare and cool.
And though I don't know much about this work, with my boots
sinking into the uncovered face of the world, I can sense
it's not how near the gulls come that bothers you.
Nor is it the near intelligibility of their cries.
It is simply how effortlessly they seem to suffer.
And wheel. And hover.

PEZ

Before Skinner and increments of reinforcement,
there was Pez. Pellets of species specific candy.
A product of the industrial revolution that put things in packages,
brought meaning to cardboard and cellophane.
Now you could get a "pack" of something.
And the stuff in the pack looked better than their ancestors,
those lumpy cigarettes you rolled by hand, or the cakes
grandma made with rumpled crusts and hunks of fruit.
I remember how an open pack of cigarettes looked like ammunition.
A line of bullets. Perfectly straight teeth.
Come to think of it, that was probably when they started
clamping down– all of a sudden everyone was wearing braces,
and smiling their big industrial smiles.
It was all part of the process.
Pez came in a dispenser. That was key.
You didn't just eat this stuff like feed from someone's hand,
but with a flick of your thumb you forged a perfect tab,
a compact block of powdered sugar emerged as if from an assembly line.
Manufactured from the force of your hand, it was not unlike
how Superman turned a lump of coal into a diamond.
It was the nearest thing to witnessing birth.
The cool thing was you could take it everywhere and be ready
for anything.
One time, after reading an essay by the young Prince Charles
about what he would take with him in the event that during a war
he was deserted on an island, my teacher asked us to write a similar essay.
She didn't tell us what the smart and practical prince put down,
and I don't remember all of what I wrote.
But I remember, I got the answers wrong.
My list, which included my bicycle and the dispenser, didn't compare.
I pictured myself on my bike, zipping from foxhole
to foxhole. With my ready dispenser, I slid between salvo
and salvo, and moment to moment.
Clearly, I was delirious.
And I think that image really bothered her.

For what could you teach someone who had
a gadget of self-reliance– a personal dispenser of candy bullion.
But I had something that she couldn't give me
and could barely control.
It's called enthusiasm.
And when I put it to good use, like not beating up my brother
or burning down the house, my parents gave me Pez.

I CALLED MY UNCLE

I called my uncle. I had something to tell him.
Out of the clear blue, he sent me five hundred dollars.
He was giving gifts to his nieces and nephews.
I was living in Binghamton, working as a substitute teacher
and living in a crappy apartment.
I didn't know if I would have work from day to day.
I didn't know why he was giving me a gift, but when I saw the check
I was grateful.
My uncle was old school. When he died, a friend referred to him
as "a diamond in the rough."
I thought about what I knew of him. He had been in World War II.
There were some stories. Hard times.
At his funeral, his brother— my dad— told a long rambling story
about how my uncle took my father to a baseball game
when my dad was young. My father stood by the grave
and recounted. He remembered that on that day the famous player,
Joe Dimaggio, hit two home runs.
It seemed like a funny story to tell at a funeral. And even more odd
was how my dad referred to the baseball player as, "Joe D."
Looking at the hole in the ground, he said,
          ".... and Joe D hit two homers."
He hesitated, as if trying to find a few more words. Nothing.
Then eventually he said, "I liked him," and took a small step back.
I wasn't sure whom my dad was referring to: the baseball player
or my uncle? And then I realized it must be my uncle— his brother.
He was talking about his brother.
It was a year earlier that I called to thank him.
I felt my uncle had looked down from somewhere and saw
where the dark was collecting in the corners and wanted
to do something for me.
When I called, I told him I wanted to thank him.
He didn't say anything.
I said it was a surprise. I listened, waiting for a response,
wondering if there were something else I could say.
That's the hard part: knowing what to say.

I imagined my father's brother in his Bronx apartment,
the way he was the last time I saw him. How he came to the door
in his underclothes and then rested in bed while we talked.
I hadn't seen him like that before.
It was the beginning of his physical decline.
Before that, he was all strength and good humor.
Now, on the phone, it was as if we were both standing in the dark.
The undivided dark that we all share, but must abide alone.
Maybe it was that that made me really feel the simplicity of his gift
and I told him I didn't think I deserved it. It was then
that the silence on the other end of the line seemed more intense.
I heard a sound like someone trying to breathe.
And then I realized, he was crying. Quietly sobbing.
Years later, after I gave a poetry reading, a friend of my father's
came up to me and shook my hand, and then he surprised me.
Holding my hand a moment longer, he said, You're not nothing.
We were standing in the doorway. I wasn't sure what he meant.
I still remember that. I didn't know, but I sensed it was meaningful .
After some time, it came to me, and I knew what to say.
Thank you, Uncle George, I said. I love you.
And before I hung up, and then for some time after, it seemed
my uncle and I were dwelling together in a timeless place.
A different place. Not this one.

MIKE

In New York freezing is about forty-two inches.
That's how far you have to dig if you're putting in a foundation.
In this case, we were digging by hand because the backhoe couldn't get in.
I'd done work like that before. One time on a farm, I had to dig
a grave for a calf. I remember I was up to my waist in the hole.
It was winter, the farmer came by, looked down and said, That's deep enough.
Another time, I was digging and found a row of horse teeth.
They were coated with dirt, but after I cleaned them off, I realized
that they weren't teeth, but a row of keys from an adding machine.
I remember holding the unearthed numbers in my hand.
They'd been in the ground for some time, but I had a feeling
they could still add.
Now it was summer and hot. Over ninety degrees.
The foreman came by. Mike. He was a good guy, but I couldn't see it.
All the others were inside, and I was out there in the heat. He picked up a shovel.
It wasn't work that a master carpenter would do but he started in.
I wasn't assuaged. I wanted to know why I was the one in the hole.
He didn't say.
I knew a little bit about him. He had graduated high school
and went right to work. By the time he was twenty five
he was an accomplished craftsman and even taught a class in construction
at the local community college. I also knew that he was recently married.
His wife, a cute but tough girl, drove motorcycles in a circus.
She was one of the riders in the round steel cage, going around and around
and upside down, held by centrifugal force.
Often there was more than one motorcycle in there.
It was really loud and smoky, and you wondered how they didn't get dizzy
or collide and crash.
Mike was in love with her. The circus was in Florida. One night she called him.
They had been going together on and off.
She was sick of it, but didn't know what to do. Mike got into his car that night
and drove twenty hours to where she was. He proposed and they came
back together.
He would talk about her.
Sometimes he would even share some of the private things they did.

Other times he talked about how he'd come home from work, tired.
She wasn't working and she was lonely and wanted to play. He told me how
he used to stop at a park on the way home sometimes and take a nap,
so that he had energy to be with her. I pictured him lying on the grass in some park.
Resting between his work life and his home life.
We were digging.   After a while, we stopped to take a drink.
The sweat was pouring off. He looked at me. I realized that he'd probably
have to go back inside, but he didn't go in. Instead he started talking.
He said that his dad died five years ago. He said that he couldn't get used to the idea
that he would never see him again. His dad would never see him with a good job
or a wife and all they were planning. I hadn't ever seen him upset.
I haven't actually seen a lot of men upset.
He said he would work for a whole year in a trench and give all his pay
if he could just see his dad for five minutes. A year of one's life for five minutes.
I tried to picture that meeting. The meeting that couldn't happen.
The truth was as flat and hot as the face of a shovel.
For a moment there was quiet. There was sadness, but it felt peaceful.
After a while, Mike went back into the house, and I went back to digging.
Back to the girl in the cage.   Back to driving all night long on the highway.

MORNING

My wife, who is often as unassuming
as Ophelia, came in last night after I had
gone to bed. Where I was? And what?
No matter. Just some lifeless golem clay,
statue that lifts under her touch and flies
to the wing of her mouth.

And she to me?
More than perpetual stasis. More than
the hard chronos that disquiets and eludes.
So much that in the monument of the dark
the hands began, and the mouths and lips
all entering into the blind drinking
and the principle of consume and be consumed
was as fine as first commission.

For is it not original what two working
the endless math of one and one can perfect,
can echo in each other?

I looked out my window this morning,
which is what writers do.
The trees were enacting their simple vigil
of absence and creation, and I thought
for a moment that would be all.

But how powerful it was then to sense
through the closed door, a drawer opening

and soon after– quiet steps on the smooth floor
and receding stair.

ERIN MURPHY

AN APPEAL TO THE POET
BEFORE THE READING

Tell me how long I have to sit here.
20 minutes? 35? God forbid, an hour?
I mean, are we talking short subway ride
bored, or Catholic funeral mass bored?
Look at the crowd: half of us are here
because we're your friends or family.
The whole back row came for extra credit.
And those proper folks up front
hope the colleague who invited you
will show up for their speakers next month.
Even if by some chance we like you –
a big *if* – we need to plan our pleasure.
Heard of those pills that give you
a four-hour erection? Trust me: leave
the party while it's in full swing.
There can be too much of a good thing.

AFTER READING A CLASSIFIED AD FOR A CAR
THAT WON'T GO IN REVERSE

Think of the metaphysics of it,
only going forward. And imagine
how you'd have to plan a day,
always parking in the back

of the supermarket lot where you
could pull ahead to a facing space,
or perhaps never stopping at all,
going to drive-thrus then looping back

like Columbus set on proving the city
round. In my dream, there is
a geyser rising under my house.
The foundation wedges itself up

like a giant loose screw
and everything begins to flow
backwards: the car in the driveway,
tiny sandbox toys—plastic tractors,

red buckets, Wiffle balls—
heating oil and water from the pipes,
all the symbols of my overstuffed
suburban life tumbling in slow motion

back toward some unknown source.
In another classified ad, someone
is willing to pay $20 for an 80s-era
Burger King kid's meal prize,

a dinosaur that *must have working wings.*
Man, I think, we live in a crazy
custom-order world and I'm afraid
I know exactly what I want.

DOES THIS POEM MAKE MY BUTT LOOK BIG?

Maybe these words   are
                    too loose
          dimply and jiggling   like cellulite
like my friend's *hind parts*
                    that can't keep
up with her girls' *bird legs*   Maybe
                    these words
          need a girdle   some wonder garment
squeezing everything
                    in its place   form-fitting   and
          corset-tight as a   quatrain
something invented by   and for
                    a man.

LIKE A FLIGHT ATTENDANT DEMONSTRATING SAFETY PROCEDURES, THE CUDDLE PARTY MODERATOR EXPLAINS THE RULES

Strangers pay $30 each to touch and embrace each other in intimate gatherings – but with strict rules forbidding hanky-panky.

—*CBS News*

Deodorant required.
No touching here.
No touching here.
No touching here.
No touching here.
No touching here.
No touching here.
No touching here.
No touching here.
No touching here.
No touching here.
No touching here.
No touching here.
Spooning encouraged.
Absolutely no forking.

244 • THE WORKING POET

SCOTLAND REVISITED

Sheep dot the hillside[1]
on the left, and on the right
the Firth of Forth[2] splays
lazily toward the horizon.
In Edinburgh, a street corner
on the Royal Mile swells
with the drone of a lone bagpiper.[3]
Here, let me take a picture
of you with the castle
in the background.[4]
Squint your eyes half-closed
for the city, the sheep
of your dreams.[5]

---

1. The backsides of the sheep are spray-painted blue, red, or green for identification purposes.

2. 'Who's on Firth?' we joke as the conductor snips our tickets.

3. His salary is paid by the Office of Tourism; the dumpster behind him is royal blue.

4. No, to the left...no, no, a little more to the right...so you'll cover the graffiti on the bridge.

5. Scientists report that insomniacs who count sheep have a harder time sleeping.

WHAT EVERY POET SHOULD KNOW ABOUT NATURAL SELECTION

When the editor
of a prestigious
British journal read
an advance copy
of Charles Darwin's
Origin of Species,
he found the focus
too narrow.
Write a book
about pigeons,
he told Darwin.
Everyone
has an interest
in pigeons.

LIZ ROSENBERG

THE JEWS (2)

The Jews in the courtyard. Slender Jewish porters carrying sol-
diers, working as human taxis. Eternal flame of the Jew's-head
lamp giving off radiance and a damp, sour smell in Argentina.
Jews on the subway, suspicious and alert. Kafka waking up feel-
ing like a bug. The Jewish man in love with a small blond
woman. Davening together like waves of the sea. Modern in silk
blouses and blue jeans, praying in the aisles of Bloomingdale's.
Bending over the forbidden water-fountain. Marching into the
ovens—a few stumbling. Jews refusing to believe this world is
paradise. Buried under the railroads of America, side by side
with Chinese. Jews run off the cliff with the Buffalo, paraded in
bloody shame beneath the Arche de Triomphe, hung by the
neck till dead in Washington Square Park, sitting *shiva* on
boxes, dyeing their hair yellow or red and fitting in. Always the
Jews—if not these Jews, then some other Jews. *Die Juden Die
Juden Die Juden*

THE USES OF ART

In dead of gloomy winter, my friend brings me a print he's made—flowers in water. I perch it on the sofa next to me, to look at, like a bird that's come close and sideways, I suddenly see faintly a yellow-green light. First light all week. Seen flashing in early spring off blossoming trees, filtered by chlorophyll. Enough lift to raise the pages of February and March, arriving half-dead at April. A happy fool.

DO SOMETHING DIFFERENT

Do something different, a friend suggests. If I could walk on
my hands all day, this might help. Head down, I would be
below notice. My feet would scan the sky.

MY FATHER, READING

His horn-rimmed glasses glinting, he sits under lamplight late into the night reading science fiction. Sometimes I come out to the den and join him. His hand dips methodically into a dish, filled with raisins, Oreos, artificial pork rinds. I think I could put cigarette butts in there, and he would eat them, automatically.

We seldom speak; he is absorbed in his book, as I am in mine. Two a.m. He returns to the kitchen cupboard, opening and closing doors, rummaging. Once in a while he says, "Listen to this," and reads a passage out loud. Once in a great while he he reads something that makes him laugh so hard tears run down his face, till he is gasping for breath. Nothing, nothing in real life affects him that way. The best I can hope for from him, with all my antics, is a sound somewhere between choking and har-rumph. After I make a joke, I can't ell if he's chuckling or clearing his throat.

Three a.m. We circle each other like lonely planets, pulled by the passionate gravity of the same sleeping sun, that woman in the dark bedroom at the other end of the house. He clears his throat, rises, closes the book. Looks at me, as if seeing me for the first time. "Isn't it getting kind of late?" he asks mildly. He walks out of the room, delicately as a cat. "Don't forget to turn out the lights," he says, exit stage left. From beyond the scrim of the room he calls back, "Good night. Sleep tight. Sweet dreams when you go to bed." He almost sings the words, same tune always. I leave the lamplight shining in the place where he sat. The glint of his folded reading glasses shines like snow on the coffee table.

THE BEAUTIFUL DAY

for my husband David

A warm, late afternoon in March.
I stay far from the shrill cry of the telephone,
the steel jaws of the mailbox.
Watch, you said yesterday, tomorrow
will be a beautiful day—
Did dawn approach you
early in her violet gown?
How do you do it day
after day after day?

IN THE HOTEL AND CONFERENCE CENTER, ON MY 40TH BIRTHDAY

Love, it is still early
—or growing very late.
Office lights across the way
stay dim with one lamp on somewhere to fool
no one, and some stranger's alarm blaring beside the bed.

The flowers still doze in their water-glass.
A few cars hum along the road.
Next time I see you
will bring more surprises,
more gifts wrapped in paper;
again the warmth of your leg over mine,
again your chest pressed to my back.
Oh demon lover,
friend and husband, father and child,
how happy it makes me
to rock in your boat another time!

JEFF SCHIFF

THE POEM AFTER ALL

in memory of Anthony Piccione

The poem after all
    is a chiseling away
        It lurks

there between the crude block
    of inattention
        & a place the gods might hallow

if only you carved them
    their rightful spot
        It is the soul of the stone

coaxed
    forward by the witting
        Praise the granite

that plummets to the floor!
    Sing mighty amens
        It is there

in the plaza *Gertrudis de Bocanegra*
    in the chill midmorning air
        finally giving

way
    to *diablito & carnitas* vendors
        & the elegant

daughters of *mestizo* shoemakers
    It is there
        in the billions of mottled

beans
    the *viejitas* sort daily
        under their tent of tarps

hunting for chaff
    for the rock
        that would find the jaw

that would destroy their livelihoods
    It is there
        after the sawdust

& filigreed pine curls
    stop
        growing at the feet of the cabinet

makers
    lining *Avenida de las Americas*
        from the foot bridge

that fords the sewage canal
    to the *Meulle General*—
        end of the watery line

land giving over to reflected sky
    The poem
        is a taking away

It can be
    nothing else
        It's what's left

after the blue milk of disaffection
    is pressed from the curds
        & the *Chihuahua cheese*

rises
    into its glassy white rinds
        It is the cooled

wax
    after the form has been hoped
        away

by the candlemaker
    It is the sweet stuff
        left

the meat of the great matter
    after the *guayaba*
        quince

mamey
    & papaya skins
        are shunted into straw baskets

& a ten peso lunch appears
    in the outstretched
        & stained hands

of your mother's mother's mother—
    sustenance
        sweeter than the soul can stand

ADIÓS

Adiós to the dumb
    straightforwardness of adobe
        Beneath scant whitewash

you are horseshit—
    compressed turds & straw
        an ancient nose

thumbed against the heat of endless days
    Adiós to the preponderance the invincibility
        the recklessness of forsythia

A trillion similes ago
    someone harnessed you
        with what they mistook for desperate

innovation:
    like a wild & golden hair
        plummeting down my lover's pliant spine

they wrote
    Adiós to the tenacious
        striated black butterflies

nearly a full notch
    above mothy aggravation
        While I am not entirely fluent

in microscopic tongues
    I spot you there
        on the burly thistle & bendy fern

Screw them & their orange world
    those monarchs & sons of monarchs
        I hear you bawling

what has become of subtle utility?
   Adiós to the *patas chicas*
      the little paws

descendants of the *Olmecs*
   the *Aztecs* the *Tarahumara*
      how I would go unshod

& disfiguringly calloused
   in your land of miniature shoes
      & outright disdain

Adiós to my days of pumping siphoning
   hauling shifting purifying
      storing & rationing water

In Mexico dear partner
   one learns
      abundance is a virtue

the rest a quaint morality—
   to which one can easily say
      adiós adiós adiós

SELF-PORTRAIT WITH FORECAST

You have a wife an appealing babe adjusting to the
face of corporeal treachery still no one's
afterthought two children: one rasping at those
outskirts that fail now to fascinate or lure &
another whose penance (when generous you call it
succor) is common distance: a furlong for every
indigestible antipathy & a mutt-Dalmatian who
trotted recently into the dangling biscuit of your
kindness & kinged you by utter mistake There is a
job: yada yada: trespasses tortured diplomacies all
the piddliness and rigmarole you'd expect from
insufficient recompense but there are laurel saplings
too: strivers oily green & sun-fuddled & quirky
hedges that demand your focus or deliberation or
depth of faith or some such amalgamated pretense
multiplying as it all does at some encroaching edge

PSALM FOR A MURDEROUS TIME

From my five arms and all my hands,
From all my white sins forgiven, they feed…
—Philip Levine

In hardass & hail the bootstrap kingdom
    In charity ends at home & ruthless evictions
        they've taught us

In my parents and parents' parents
    managed straight off the boat
        seven to a bed shoeless gaunt night

& day peddling streetcorner thin air
    yams and bobbins needle work hod work
        suet in the swinging tenement pail

fifth floor walkup why can't you they've taught us
    In there's never
        don't buy that godly twaddle

plenty for everymotherson
    they've taught us
        Rein in hunker down keep kin close

they've taught us
    In we've done ours goddamit
        pony you up belly you up

eye on the keep plugging
    it's bound to happen
        In many have perished

and those with everything to lose
    save yourself they've steel yourself they've
        taught us

sleep fast against every ramrod bolted door

SPITS BLOOD

He who hears this name (God) from a Jew must inform the authorities, or else throw sow dung at him when he sees him and chase him away.
—*Martin Luther*

Bless me
    for I have thus far survived
        my birthright—

kike killer of Christ
    Bless me
        for I've understood

pain makes you no more famous
    than pity
        that none should run headlong

toward either
    Bless me
        for I've learned

we loathe what we consider least
    or worst
        Bless me

for I know we are redeemed
    by foregoing redemption
        Bless me

for I was twelve once
    on the first day of the New Year
        5729

head lashed by a neighborhood wind
    for the endless length
        of 58th Avenue and Hollis Court Blvd

velvet skullcap prayer shawl
    phylactery case
        swept under my left arm

Bless me
    for I was twelve years later
        and twice that age

accosted in the ignorant Midwest
    disgust
        and Roman confusion

rising
    in the rasp sneer of my accuser
        Bless me for I did not

now
    or ever
        staple

the Lord God His Son Proxy
    or salvation of any sort
        to a whittled tree

Bless me
    for though you are the first I'm telling
        the country the banished

inherit
    is no more frightening
        than dirt

THE HOMILY OF INFINITUDE

I was digging with my fingernails, trying to join the dead in that grave…
but the grave would not open…. I cried out to my mother, my father,
"Why did they not kill me? What was my sin?"
—Rivka Yosselevska

Better a living death than a dead life.
—Rabbi Moshe Chaim Lau

&

My grandfather is puny
   no larger than a doubt
      veiled forty years

He was not wrenched
   from wife and child
      in the *Umschlagplatz*

by teenage conscripts
   who met his entreaties
      with rifle shots to the groin

His beard and sidelocks
   were not torn from his face
      by carousing gendarmes

who demanded he recite
   the 26th Psalm or croon
      his anthem of hope the *Hatikvah*

at full voice
   He did not choose
      to terminate the unendurable

at the mouth's end
   of a stolen pistol
      moments before the *Einsatzkommando*

would have surely done the same
   though in the name
      of quite a different Lord

He was no
   scribe merchant or petty
      official in Odessa

October 23rd 1941 herded
   then doused with benzene and immolated
      behind barricaded factory doors

He did not gag
   slowly on carbon monoxide
      or Cyclon B

while sealed
   in a gas lorry dieseling
      through dense Polish woods—

"even in death you could tell
   the families, all holding hands"
      He is slight

but was not de facto
   a subject of empirical studies on starvation
      performed behind the Warsaw wall

by thirty-three starving *Galitzianer* physicians
   who too would wither
      but leave for the record

their worthwhile efforts
   He did not sanctify *The Name*
      martyred while battling

in the *Zydowska Organzarja Bojowa*
   He did not witness
      his wife's uterus

filled to hemorrhage
 with pure carbolic malarial parasites
  or white cement-like fluid

"by means of an electrically driven pump"
 He did not stand desperate
  lamenting & astonished

as 300 boxcars of used undergarments
 eyeglasses crutches and prostheses
  arrived from the *Chelmno* camp

for recycling
 He was not forced
  to copulate with gypsy women

in the sight of clergy and *landsleit*
 He did not clamber
  during cover of night

from the freshly limed pits
 at *Babi Yar*
  the shoulders of infanticide

his only foothold to freedom
 His testicles
  were not champed repeatedly

by specially trained Ukrainian hounds
 as he strode the *Himmelfahrstrasse*
  toward sure asphyxiation-——

alternately reciting *Viddui* and *Kaddish*
 the litany of confession
  and the litany of mourning

He did not perish
 upright in the cattle wagons
  en route to *Treblinka*

with "even healthy, young, strong organisms"
    nor was hoisted or fed
        through a transom or barred window

on to the already corpse-littered rails
    His was not the choice
        of daughter or father mother or son

links und rechts useful versus useless
    at the *Birkenau* siding—
        children swung like sacks like puppets

into lampposts wagon wheels
    into steel footings
        children gored in rucksacks

market bags through pillow cases
    children hurled on to bayonets
        or bashed into pulp

with surplus steel chain
    He was not appointed
        to sort segregate classify

for the Booty Store
    hammer and extract
        dental fillings

harvest hair
    or locate gems secreted in toothpaste
        in vaginal openings sewn in skin

He did not dream
    three years of headlong death
        in horsestall or hayloft

on the outskirts
    of *Vilna Bialystok Radom*
        He was not condemned

to stand naked all night
    in subzero weather
        in a water barrel

at the *Janowska* Road camp
    for the crime of not looking clean enough
        nor did he succumb elsewhere

to typhus typhoid fever cholera
    dysentery or "endemic swellings"
        nor expire from phenol injections to the heart

He did not ingest
    electrified wire while scrabbling
        toward rainwater

pooled around a Lager latrine
    He is tiny true
        but did not peddle

his anus in *Auschwitz* for two rations
    of maggoty bread
        saltless hot water beetroot bits of nettles

and one of malignant kohlrabi mush
    or barter his mouth
        for half that

He was not forced to dance
    through thigh-deep offal
        wrapped in ceremonial shawl

while those who watched and waited
    listened to *Drei Lilien*
        and were denied even the hope

of *holyswiftmerciful* murder
    Miniature
        At times he hardly draws air

But his is not among
    the fingernail signatures
        entered on the low ceiling

of the bade und *inhalationsraume*
    His eyes do not protrude
        from their sockets "as if

they were two superfluous items
    detached from the face"
        His skull was not among

those "dipped in preservative liquid,
    and put in a specially prepared
        hermetically sealed tin"

for the advancement of Aryan science
    He is not
        human tar say bonesap or creosote

caked on the ties
    between Rotterdam
        and *Oswiecim* stations

He is not soap lather
    on the scrotal sack
        of an Austrian miner

able finally to earn his livelihood
    without bloodsucking Semitic labor lawyers
        He is not a clot

of human smoke unearthed
    during autopsy
        in the left ventricular wall

of a stillborn Bavarian boychild
    His forearm
        is not blued with the *gematria*

of the living-already-dead
    nor did he learn the homily of infinitude
        at *Sobibor Belzec*

Buchenwald Dachau Ravensbruck
    He was not seized rounded up loaded
        evacuated methodically resettled mobilized

shunted transported emigrated elsewhere
    nor hunted driven bludgeoned lashed
        "scourged with leaden whips rubber clubs

and all kinds of flagellation instruments"
    nor tattooed selected shorn shocked
        castrated by X-rays gassed incinerated

hanged drowned
    "systematically murdered
        according to preconceived plan"

He is not one six-millionth part
    of a German Polish Estonian
        French Czech Rumanian or Dutch

wagonload heap mass
    swelling hillock mound ditch
        or sodgrave of Jews

He is slight
    yet has outlasted
        those he knew as a boy at prayer

or bathing in the river *Warta*
    and those he knew for wit
        horse sense piety song

and those he did not know
    or have anything to do with
        but were all the same

children of the covenant
  He is not a fluke of survival
    owing his life to cunning

deception betrayal
  He dwindles yes but does not
    dust himself with ash daily

and traipse idly through the streets—
  damn be his unwitting resolve
    He is small—almost without form—

though his teeth are not banked
  and preserved in archival
    black-and-white footage

but still pulverize an apple
  and tear its flesh
    and forcefully extract essence

each morning in Miami Beach
  His wife yet drills
    her full bosom into his chest

as they rumba and cha-cha
  on the terrace of the Eden Roc
    Small

Still he often turns to survey
  his life in sweeping lines
    on and off axis:

home and family four generations
  happily in tact
    and prosperous

Because he was not one
  who would "simply fall away
    and leave the earth a cleansed place"

Because only the slain
    are whole and beyond doubt
        my grandfather shrinks withers

often occupying less space
    than a sealed eyelid
        or lips clamped around

an ever-stifled shriek

JOHN STIGALL

UP IN DIXIE

I grew up in Dixie
during the nineteen fifties & sixties, attended
negro schools and a nonviolent colored church. The grocery
stores always stocked pork
& beer & white bread & cigarettes
& lard. Even Uncle Ben smiled for something
white & good for you. Aunt Jemima never saw grits
as offensive as that
little defiant nappy headed
nephew who definitely wasn't going to live
long because he had trouble
grinning & saying "Yes Sir" to Jesus-figures, good
ole boys, or anybody who wasn't willing
to dowse the flames of a burning cross
on a dare. In spite
of stares & sighs, signs & whispers, &
neighborhoods we could only enter
safely during daylight hours to clean, mow,
or rake—I loved
being in a world where
a glance was a s deadly as a stare
& a prayer as militant as a dream.

I grew up in Dixie, learned hatred
can be pleasant, cultural, & ordained—especially
if no mention is made of
notches or buckles
in the Bible belt
& the Lord's name is used
before saying grace
or damn

THAT SABBATH MORING AT EPHESUS

After a wild night of drunken heathen sedition
on Lenox Avenue
I quietly entered the sanctuary
at Ephesus
to persuade the Spirit.   I was drawn
                        to a still
                            small
silence
a young woman expressed.   I drew
near her, quietly; & along with her
& the congregation I knelt, quietly, in prayer.
Although I listened

I do not believe

I heard the minster's sermon,
nor can I recall being drawn
to confess by the sermon's appeal. But I can
say this though,
            Her eyes were brown as the dust of Eden's
            ground, & her flesh was blacker and clearer than
Gethsemane's sky That seditious night.
And although I never met her, I can still
faithfully say
            I know I will
never pray again
like I did that Sabbath morning
in the presence of such silent beauty

DECEMBER/JANUARY

There are some people
who you just cannot
speak to
or wave at
or look at
when they stare
you down. I cannot
speak to
or even wave at
passing
taxi cab drivers
because they stop.

Southern policemen are the same way

except I don't have to
speak, wave, or stare

before they stop

INTO THE LIFE OF THIS WORLD

I.

At thirty-five, too young to be sickened
in the light, my father's
body—perfect, calm—forms a fetal
curl about its silent agony. His eyes, suggestive
& articulate, explain. The light
wanes

II.

   Silent, I refuse the first breaths (cradled in
       the light). My
  body—stillborn, calm, numb from the canal—appears
  deaf, dumb.

See the physician & my mourning mother
curl over me, warping my flesh, weeping,
praying me into the life of this world

IN THE BIBLEBLACK AIR

The city squints,
face by face,
in the bibleblack air.
I stare,
blankly, lean
from my shoulders,

    & weigh.
City nights do not sleep. They slowly toss,
turn, squint, turn, toss, pause,
    & weigh.

Soul by soul
in the bibleblack air,
the city stares.
I squint,
slowly, pause
in my silence,

    & weigh

ANNIE

Your perfume led me
to you. I was young &
drunk off my
ass. You were
waiting.

I picked you
up. We drank.
Swayed like trees in the wind.
We fucked.

I heard you
were picked up
again—

This time
you were waiting
in a large
plastic bag.

They say you waited a week, Annie.

Your perfume led,
led the search.

A mop protruded,
hung like a wreath.

PHIL TERMAN

FROM *THE USED CAR LOT*

1. One Day This Will All Be Yours

I don't fall in love
with any of them, my father says,
his back hunched
over the titles on his desk,
the butt-end of a cigar

he can't smoke at home
torn as a crumpled dollar bill.
During the riots
the place was torched,
the neighborhood clogged

like arteries
in the year of the heart attack.
Now, pennants hanging from wires
in rows above the cars
cough dust into Cleveland humidity.

My father tells me to wash
the frontline, claims
I think manual labor
is a Mexican. A customer arrives,
looks over a brown Dodge.

It's good transportation, he says.
He sold one without an engine once.
I hose a hood
clean of pollution
that splotches everywhere.

Back in the office, over gin rummy,
my father sweeps his eyes
over his rented property:
One day this will all be yours.
He picks up the gut card

I throw him, places it gently
into his spread, slides it down
with his elbow, pauses,
and gins.
Didn't I tell you never to speculate?

3. Our Only Guarantee

The cars face Euclid Avenue
in uneven rows,
wise in their junk frames.

The bodyman wheels them in,
removes rust, spray paints,
assigns each a place:

in front—'68 Pontiac,
'73 Olds, '66 Caddy,
pink, with A.C.,

'80 Mustang with music,
in back—the junkers
that won't turn over,

weeds jetting out of fenders,
hoods, trunks, doors, open to give
one more spare part: jack and hubcap,

radiator and radio.
Each is priced *As Is*.
Our only guarantee is to the curb.

Used and sold, used and sold,
spun down countless highways,
driven beyond their limits,

stalled, abandoned
just after breakdowns,
how did they congregate

in this gravel yard
like pilgrims gathered
at the Holy Land?

5. The Last of the Hippies

Jesse the bodyman. a pimp on the side, makes the cars hum,
in the greasy garage, windowless, tires stacked to the tilting
point, country music blasting from the transistor, the toilet
backed up, *Playboy* centerfolds shaping the dust, tools haphaz-
ard on the cracked cement floor.

"Get you any woman you want," he says, but seventeen, I
sneak phone calls to my girlfriend or lay on the black vinyl
couch reading *The Brothers Karamazov,* my father shuffling
through car titles on hi desk: "Go watch Jesse," he'd say, "You
might learn something. Go screw in a plate."

Having to go to the bank, he puts me in charge, shows me a
list with two columns scrawled in pencil, one marked, "preferred
price," the other "lowest we'll go."

"Back in a few minutes," and no sooner he's out the door, he
pauses: "If you get any customers, try to hold them until I get
back. Stall them—show them around, start a few cars."

Humid afternoon, air all haze, trash stench form the next
door MacDonalds, Euclid Avenue screaming, one way down—
town, one way the suburbs—my spirit sweating to escape, and
Fyodor Karamazov murdered just as a customer arrives all muscle
and mirror sunglasses: "I want the Ford in back." My father
told me stories about criminals on the lam needing cars in a
hurry. He didn't mind: "They always pay up front, cash." As
usual, this junker needs a charge-up: the man twitches, Jesse

wheels the gigantic battery charger over, cracks the hood, tightens the wires—it juices right up, and I feel the damp of hundreds and fifties; the customer peels out like a drag racer.

My first sale! This long-haired distracted son my father calls *The Last of the Hippies* is worthy and the old man will be proud; he is, he pats me on the back, offers me a cigar, claims in a puff of smoke I'll inherit the business, demonstrates the most important sales tactic: "If a customer looks at a car, don't approach immediately. If he bickers with the price, look him in the eyes and walk away, just walk away," straightening himself by way of demonstration as my customer returns, steaming as the hot sidewalks, blood-faced, pounding his fist on the desk, demanding his money—he turned the engine off and it won't restart.

My father doesn't look up, cocksure: Sorry, sir. We sell our cars *as is*." I bury my nose deep in the ravings of Ivan Karamazov to the Grand Inquisitor. "This box here," my father mutters, staring at the form a second too long. "Well, I see it isn't checked," pointing to me. "He sold you the car, didn't he? Well, look at him." Both glare at me as they would a disobedient dog. "He doesn't know nothing."

Later. at home over dinner, my father snips sharply: "How can you be such a *mishugenah?* What do you want to be, anyway?

"A writer and a teacher."

"I'm glad," he fires back, biting down on his steak as if it was the word and not the piece of meat he was ferociously chewing, "you didn't say: *poet*."

CODA: MY FATHER CALLS MY NAME
IN THE VOICE OF A BIRD

A bird I can't identify
cries from the next field
its two notes: *Phil-up,*

Phil-up, the way my father
would caterwaul my name
up the stairs for supper.

I still hear him, though
from the other world,
clamor for me to gather

in the feasting. If so,
it would be Sunday night
and the steak medium rare,

sautéed with onions,
fried potatoes on the side.
It was his meal

as far of heaven
as in his life he'd believe.
He taught us to suck the meat

clean of the bone.
But what if these echoes
have nothing to do

with my father and me?
What if the bird is exclaiming
its own hunger from the spruce

and, as is most likely, sounds
like a familiar voice only because
I want, like everyone,

for my beloved dead to live again?

THE SHVITZ

If the *Torah* is our lives,
our portion was sung in that sanctuary
of a steamhouse by a *minyan* of ten
thirteen-year-old boys and a counselor,
a secular rabbi who knew the streets
like an emissary from the world
where our lives are already sealed.

He led us past the sign that still reads
members only, listed in the phone book
as *The Russian Bath and Tea Room,*
but known to initiates as *Sweat*
in Yiddish, on 116th and Luke, our parents'
old neighborhood when all the world
was kosher and on Sabbath mornings

they walked in tennis shoes under
laundry drying above the street,
past houses of uneven boards
and sunken roofs, the fishmarket,
the famous Zeiger's Delicatessen,
before it changed, all except this small
brownstone, with a *mezuzah* on the door.

In front of the lockers I imitated his motions
as he took off his suit coat, muscles bulging
behind white shirt and tie, his pants,
the undershirt, the underwear, and I was afraid
to go on, to show myself in front of strangers.
Come on, he said, *here we're all the same,*
underneath. Once, late at night,

just we two gave each other backrubs
on his living room floor. My shoulder blades
felt like wings beneath his moist palms
as he rubbed down my back and around
the inside of my arms, kneading
my flushed skin with his fingertips.
I was one body touching another body.

Here, cots with clean sheets lined
the central room. He instructed: *After*
we sweat, we rest. Adjacent, the dining area:
kosher pickles and hot peppers in bowls
under a photograph of the Wailing Wall:
After we rest, we eat. Steaks with garlic
broiled in the stove. *Then we go sweat some more.*

We were with history.
But all we knew was that we were naked
among men who were reading newspapers
or talking about how it was all changing
and the law was in our hands.
Our counselor led us into the steamroom
where old men sat on towels beside buckets

of cold water they'd pour over their heads
and fill up again. We began at the lower
bench, facing the hole in the wall where
the sandstones glowed like burning bushes,
then moved up, rising with the heat, daring
the others to lie full length at the top,
long as they could stand it, longer,

until the room was so full of gray mist
we became outlines of figures floating
in a secluded room, simmering out
all of our small tensions, and still he'd say:
Throw in more water, it's not hot enough—
our heads down, my hands, like his, gripping
splintered wood against the oncoming rush.

ALBERT EINSTEIN AT THE SOUP KITCHEN

Do I look like anyone? he asks,

as he swoops the long spoon into the peas,
lifts it a few inches
and holds it steady to pour
onto the tray of the next famished mouth,
shouts to George for more
as his supply empties down.

I'm the bread and donut man
in this assembly line of volunteers
who gather for our three hours
of weekly service and socialism:

Jose the finger pointing Filipino
who pours the punch and repeats:
The wages of sin is death,
and only reads Paradise from the Comedy,

for his description of heaven, he says, *and light;*

Jake the Buddhist, who scrapes the dishes
as they are returned, saves whatever
appears untouched for someone else's

insatiable hunger:
        Sal, who tells me he was on the other side
of the line, meaning he was one of the thousand
who form every morning single-file around this Church
of the Apostles, up 9ᵗʰ Avenue and around

28ᵗʰ Street,
        like the snake, he chants,
looking out the window beyond Crack Park,

cursed above the beasts of the city
to eat dust all the days of its life.

And their eyes are filled with dust,
                              drugged and sleepy,
bodies stiff from sidewalk cardboard sofas.

The peaman, it turns out, looks like Albert Einstein,
the shaggy white hair and white mustache,
pronounced nose and dark sad eyes.

I'm an actor, he explains. *They pay me to look like the genius.*

he shows me his card: $e=mc^2$:
Equity equals many characters,

and I'm honored to be near even the resemblance of the man—
not because I understand relativity
and the contradicting theories of light,

but because of how steady he is with the spoon,
filling each helping to the brim,
as if each portion should be equal and abundant.

ALTERNATIVE TEN COMMANDMENTS

Thou shalt walk with your love on summer evenings before
supper to the pond with the many peepers.

Thou shalt sit in silence and listen to deep-throated trills
chorusing their frog spirits from homes of leaves and
sticks and water.

Thou shalt observe the gradual emergence of the Big Dipper,
star by star.

Thou shalt not long for anywhere else.

Thou shalt clear the mind of affairs of business and duty.

Thou shalt look from the ground to thy lover's face, and press
your lips there, and your tongue, and open your face to
your lover's lips and tongue.

Thou shalt not be afraid of flashing lights and deer spotters and
broken pick-ups.

Thou shalt slowly rise, and bopping to the frog's song, shimmy
to the pond until the wheat field swallows your shadow.

Thou shalt fulfill the frog's longing and make your bodies bare,
and slide into the water and glisten.

Thou shalt remain until your heartbeats slow down, and the
moon appears above the surface.

Appendices

EDWARD DOUGHERTY

APPRENTICE DAYS

Heart Speaks to Heart

It was not a desk. Six handmade wooden crates, stacked two each. Two pine boards going one way, a single one spanning the other, making two sides of a square which I stepped into. It wasn't an office, but it was a workspace. Along one wall, the bench with pegboard was idle and mostly storage. There, I placed some way of filling the air with music. That was always my first order of business wherever and whenever I moved. Set up tunes: receiver, turntable, tape player, run speaker wire. The components have shrunk over the past twenty five years, but the presence of music has not. I probably got the stereo going even before unpacking the crates, leveling the planks with wads of folded paper, or carefully placing the glass desktop. In the shadows alongside the stairs stood the mechanical organs of the house: furnace and water heater. When I graduated from college with my degree in English, a Creative Writing major and a minor in Religious Studies, I moved into my parents' home and established my "study" in the basement. Even though I envisioned myself a Poet while at Penn State, I count that year at that desk my first writer's space as Year One in my apprenticeship as a writer.

There's no reason anyone should read on. As Emily Dickinson said, "I'm nobody."

I even had to quote her to say that.

In publishing terms, I still aspire to work my way up to becoming a mid-list poet. Like thousands of writers, I've published a couple of books and some chapbooks that few have heard of, fewer have read. I have at least five manuscripts in my files, unpublished, errr, I mean "looking for a publisher." I don't get invitations for my work, let alone my presence at conferences or reading series. And yet, isn't that the state of things for the majority of us? Most writers are nobodies. Framing the issue in marketing terms is false. I suspect even those who have household names can shout

"Amen!" when Dickinson says, "How dreary to be somebody!" She says it's "like a frog / To tell your name the livelong day / To an admiring bog!" One *New Yorker* cartoon put it this way, "Sure, he can type the type but can he hype the hype?"

For all writers, the work is what's essential. And that requires becoming a person. From that struggle and in our anonymity, we reach out to each other. Right after declaring her nobody status, Dickinson asks, "Who are you? / Are you nobody, too?" Learning the craft of writing, for me, has been a way to grow in authenticity. And it always starts in the silence of our own private frog-pond, or in my case, parents' basement.

I have kept journals since eighth grade, poured out heartfelt letters and love notes all through high school, even writing poems, mocking teachers and imitating textbook samples. I declared my major in English from the first week in State College, where I took up both the Creative Writing option and the Education component because, hey, you need something to fall back on, right? With an insight I still don't understand, I saved workshops for when I'd read through my survey courses. But I thought of myself as a writer. More importantly, to me anyway, I thought of myself as a poet. An Artist. I went barefoot to classes, carrying flip-flops in my backpack. I conformed to the extent of wearing them indoors. I sat under elm trees, reading: Thomas Merton and others on Christian contemplation, D. T. Suzuki's take on Zen, Wordsworth, T. S. Eliot, and E. E. Cummings—I wanted to perceive the heart of things. I wanted to be a mystic. Maybe all I wanted was to show how "sensitive" and "deep" I was. Maybe I had all of that going on, but I certainly didn't know how to craft the language or my own life to merge perception with expression. I was too busy venting and emoting.

After graduation, I gradually wrote less and less until I don't think I was writing very much at all. In my final semester, I'd taken three writing courses and whatever else I was studying surely required papers. I was tired. I also had to move, get a job (*gasp!*), and begin managing in earnest the details of mature life. I owe a great debt to my father and mother who got me through college without saddling me with financial debt (and I was the seventh of eight to be so fortunate), who set me up with a used car as a gift (again, freeing me from further debt), and who welcomed me back into their house. I wasn't the only one who needed additional support in this way, coming from a big Catholic family, but I knew even then that being a poet is no moneymaker. Managing the "worldly affairs" of a life of art would be another hallmark of my apprenticeship. But first I needed a "life of art" to balance with whatever else I was supposed to manage.

In the months after graduating, I wrote some poems over the summer and early fall, but soon the habit dropped away. So many beginning writers say they don't write much when they're happy, but give us depression! Give us anger! Give us the sweet flavor of feeling misunderstood! Then, words avalanche out of us, crashing loudly, unstoppable force. In my post-graduation period of silence, I questioned whether I *was* a poet. Maybe I only wrote because it had been assigned. Maybe it was yet another way of expressing, not a deep need within me, but a powerful desire to please others, to live up to their expectations.

I got a job at *The Cable Guide*, customizing the monthly magazine so viewers could program their VCRs accurately. We formed a creative bunch with many antics. But mostly that first year was shaped by my relationship with M, and our yearlong passion. We'd met at Penn State and moved within miles of each other outside of Philly. Each week, as we chose our destinies, as we chose to embody our values and personalities, we grew apart. Her degree in physics (along with her remarkable hard work and her startlingly acute mind) secured a fistful of job offers; she had accepted her position with GE even before we graduated. My English degree (and my penchant for "spontaneity,") did not open employment doors in quite the same way. She bought furniture (new) to fill out her first apartment; I arranged copy-paper boxes for my bureau in college then after graduation I used my childhood furniture. Because of her security clearance, she could not tell me about her work at GE; not likewise limited, I held forth about the Pax Christi meetings seeking peace, in part through protesting GE's defense research. She could see into her professional future; I wasn't willing to plan our weekends. She thought I was "too Bohemian" and I thought she was remarkably acute. When we broke up, further silences emerged in my own life. I turned to literature. I returned to my own roots.

I began with William Pratt's *The Imagist Poem* and Mary Barnard's translation of Sappho, I turned to Rexroth's versions of Chinese and Japanese poems. Listening to George Winston, William Ackerman, or other acoustic instrumentals, I discovered how poetic words can be as full of energy as the classic rock I was reared on. The concentration of feeling in such literature resonated with my own heartbreak, but I loved how experiences hundreds of years apart spoke to each other. I also picked up the Gary Snyder volumes he signed when he came to Penn State, but whom I was too shy to actually speak to, though he sat in on our workshop. Reading his poems in this context, I felt a different relationship to my own landscape peeking up in my heart like a seedling. *Cor ad cor loquitor*, Cardinal Newman wrote. *Heart speaks to heart.* With such company, I didn't feel so alone in the world. My silences were filling with purpose and the community of writers, a community not bound by time or geography.

Down in my basement study, practicing calligraphy, I lettered those tiny poems, letting their images develop in my mind as I had to slow my mind down to lay down each stroke within each letter. I savored the lines, word by word. I relearned the principles of the Imagists, particularly the authoritative authority, Ezra Pound. I began writing description, striving to notice the subtle changes in daily light and seasonal shifts, but also striving to use fewer and fewer words. Well, not exactly. It was never a countable thing. If a phrase isn't needed, cut it, or if something could be said more economically, do it. But the discipline goes beyond such mechanical concerns. When I copied Sappho's or ancient Japanese poems, by hand, a practice I maintain to this day, I couldn't articulate what I was hoping for. What I didn't understand yet was that I love these kinds of poems because they evoke much from as few words as possible. There is a vastness to them, out of proportion to their printed scale. At their best, the concentrated image rises above mere description to meaning. Describing *things* allows inner states to be situated in the world so that the seemingly stable outer world gains the fluidity of emotional forces, personalizing it, while the individual's experience gains the context of the impersonal flow of nature.

With evenings and weekends free, a job that was a draining kind of busywork, I spent many hours in that basement. I'd lived underground in college (and later in grad school) since those apartments are cheapest, so the dark and the yellow buzz of fluorescent lighting were familiar, comforting. Most crucially, I was maintaining a productive solitude, a deep-down friendliness with myself, the person I wake to each morning and fall asleep with each night. Harmonious companionship with one's own self is utmost in any person's life, but especially an artist, since it is out of the sheer mountainside of the heart that all true art springs.

Throughout that year, I saved up money and planned two events. I set time aside for a two part vacation and then when I came back, I'd give my notice to the *Cable Guide*: the first week I'd fly out west, and the second, I'd go on retreat. The trip west was to Seattle to visit a former *Cable Guider* who loved to haunt used bookstores, with a side trip to "meet" my cousin, Kate, living in a cabin by the Pacific, north of San Francisco. I'd only recently learned that Kate was a poet. This was like discovering gravity: a family member who *understands!* The world makes sense after all! We began a correspondence that I am still enriched by. I'd fly from Seattle to San Francisco, rent a car, visit Kate, and before heading back to Seattle, I'd go to City Lights Books. It'd be like a pilgrimage. It was a pilgrimage.

When I got home, I'd take a weeklong silent retreat in Maryland, where I'd been on retreats all through college. My Catholic angel-wrestling about becoming a Christian Brother is a different apprenticeship story, but at this point I was still on the horns of my lifelong dilemma: a life of literature or a life of service/ministry? The question was should I pursue a Masters in social work of some kind or should I go for an MFA in creative writing? These twin journeys helped begin unknotting that false polarity and set me on my discipleship as a writer.

Questions of Preparation

What's an apprentice need to learn? Between the first inklings about being a writer and through the many pages of what later is called "juvenilia," there is a period of formation that prepares for a life of writing. So what preparation is needed? What skills need to be honed? What knowledge is foundational? If the writing community knew the answers to this, there would be fewer how-to books, and if the academic community knew the formula, there would be less discrepancy in the types of writing programs—graduate, undergraduate, post-graduate, conference-for-credit, low-residency—and there'd be more similar orientation and foci.

Because "writing" is such a vast set of formal constructions with too many intended audiences to reduce to a simple formula, there's no way to standardize. Then there's the variable of the individual writer. I speak for the nobody I am, hoping the questions we entertain and the forces we engage with are similar enough. Each of us struggles to address questions of craft and of self, of the technical and mundane methods and of the philosophical elements. If we're lucky, these questions never resolve themselves completely or for long.

What are the forms I am most able to write in? What forms should I challenge myself to learn? How do I find and can I be found by ideas? How do I keep track of my submissions? What writers are my exemplars? What's a dangling modifier? How do I make a life of writing and maintain healthy relationships? What is "voice" and have I found mine? What do I do with all these files, drafts, clippings, binders, and computer files? If I have an audience, how do I reach them? If I don't, how do I cultivate one?

In my work doing retreats, I used Rilke's advice to the young poet to be patient with all that is unresolved in one's heart and to love the questions, not the answers. In fact, he says, don't worry about the answers because you're not ready for them; instead, live the questions. While I was conscious of this effort to remain patient and to live the quest, I was not conscious of these exact writing concerns in my apprentice days. I just kept plucking along, unaware that I'd learned all that much until several events in 2005 helped me reflect. Only in retrospect—from the vantage point of nearly twenty years later—did I realize that I was no longer a beginner. Between the two was this story, which begins with Denise Levertov.

Form and Work

Flying home from my pilgrimage to my one known relative who not only appreciated poetry but who wrote it herself, I read the two authors my cousin Kate recommended. I'd bought Robert Bly's translation of Rilke's poetry and Denise Levertov's *The Poet in the World*. In "Some Notes on Organic Form," Levertov's words struck the hollow of my secret intuitions, and they resonated with a truth that not only confirmed my experience but has been a source of musing ever since. She starts with a seemingly innocuous statement that behind her conception of organic form in poetry is the idea that "there is form in all things (and in our experience) which the poet can discover and reveal." Artistic creation is not separate from nor in essence different from any other creation. More than a fascinating concept to mull over while pulling my chin, such a conviction establishes a person's stance toward the world and experience, providing a meaningful continuity and a way to engage with it.

For some artists, the world of things and relations is chaotic, but through Protean effort the artist shapes the formless. Novelists know that life has no narrative arc, is full of extraneous details that no writer should leave in, and has been crammed with too many characters, and so the writer creates or at least transforms the meaningful bits so that they contribute to the revelation of personality, relationship, or action. However, Levertov's idea says that there is meaning and shapeliness in our interactions, and so rather than willful creation, the artist needs receptivity most. A seemingly meaningless chat by the punch bowl at a company holiday party could bear within it the detail that reflects the many dimensions of a co-worker's life. Striving for this kind of attentiveness, I wrote a poem about a receptionist's face as she answered the phone on the anniversary of her son's death—it was exactly the mix of routine and humdrum with the profound and emotional that I understood as the form I needed to acknowledge and honor. My stance toward experience has a genuflection in it.

Levertov illuminates her notion of innate form with an image, comparing the coalescing impressions that give rise to the language of a poem to a "constellation," which struck me a perfect metaphor. Better than "coalescing," certainly. I can imagine that I leaned my head back and gazed out the little plane window at the landscape or the cloudscape below, considering how this constellating occurs in my own life. It happens all the time. And still does. While reading, a lively phrase or startling impression expands in my mind beyond the confines of the page and often evokes emotions connected to completely separate experiences. Then, like stars that may be light-years apart, these varied and disassociated sensations take on a perceivable shape in relation to each other. For example, catching the sunset through silhouetted trees in autumn once during my commute during these years, I recalled a news story about the number of children who die a day of malnutrition, and the third "star," the experience that showed the outline of the poem was the melancholy of autumn, that particular sadness of evening that edges on rage. Or: flipping through a book of artwork, I sense the boundaries of the self blurring as I gaze at a Seurat, as if the man made of dots is my own personality, my own mixture of dark and light, muted and pure, and the language that emerges uses "I" but not the details of my life. Or: vague leftover dream images of a train station, which have shed the story as well as the meaning (if I knew it) of the dream itself, but the image of the wood planks combines with remembered trips on the SEPTA trains and the imagined stance of my father on his commute into Philadelphia. This constellation could still be compelling enough and so, as Levertov says, it "wakes in [the poet] this demand: the poem."

Rather than waiting on sufficiently "poetic" experiences or reserving writing for when emotions are overflowing so powerfully that I *must* write, Levertov says that paying attention to subtler influences may induce the same "demand." This new orientation marks a tidal shift of perception, one that many beginning writers do not make, especially poets. It moves from an understanding of writing as a means of expression to a means of discovery. Beginning with a description of the train station and ending with a poem about my father is unexpected, unpredictable, and exhilarating.

To engage in this process of attending to the liminal interaction between outer experience and inner impression, I took instruction from Rainer Maria Rilke's own example. He transitioned from poems of feeling (*The Book of Hours,* for example) to books of *things,* published in the two collections of *New Poems* from 1907 and 1908. And his mentor was the sculptor Auguste Rodin. Even now I have the image of Rodin pacing his studio as assistants worked on various components of *The Gates of Hell,* so perhaps one was polishing downward-pointing hands of *The Three Shades,* who overlook the suffering contained in those monumental doors; another was shaping the leaning back of *The Thinker* who ponders the scene also from above. Meanwhile, the master threads through all this activity, supervising, and as he does so, he takes clay in his hands, shaping it, and lays small figures here and there among all this production. Always working. How much of this is romanticized, half-remembered and half-created, I don't know, but the spirit of this artist motivates me to this day. When Rilke became Rodin's secretary, the poet asked how he might improve his writing practice, how does an artist come up with material for his art? *"Travailler, travailler, travailler!"* shouted Rodin. Not by musing or waiting on inspiration, but "work, work, work." He suggested that the poet learn to observe things, not just look at them, but learn to see. "Go to the zoo," he instructed, "and observe the animals. Two to three weeks might not be enough."

The enterprise of learning to see a panther, for example, or a grasshopper, or the twist of hair on a woman's neck, or the changing light on a marble angel's wing—as Rilke's own poems were doing—took me to a continuing education class in drawing. I drew my hand, my guitar case, a jar of pencils, a rock on my desk. The objects themselves didn't make the artwork, I quickly realized, but the quality of the technique. Craft, not feeling. The material is as important as the content. I continued exploring the effects of linebreaks and imagery, and now I knew I had to go deeper—yes, work more on the craft of poems, but I also had to learn how to shape my life to do that work.

Candles in the Hatband

The lives of artists were instructive. Rodin's example for Rilke continued but I also learned how Cezanne created a two-dimensional patterning on canvas even while suggesting three-dimensional landscapes or how Van Gogh embodied his feeling in the thickness of paint and measure of brushstroke. From these biographies, I also learned the work of hauling your easel out into the open air to paint the mountain in storm-shadow and morning light, as Cezanne did, or to stick candles in your hatband to paint after dark, as Van Gogh did. "Work, work, work."

I subscribed to *The Writer's Digest*, which still features articles on how to characterize your villain in a detective story alongside how to write a query letter to an editor to get a contract for an article project, and get paid for it. Story after story chronicled the leap from paid work into the unknown of freelance writing, the difficulties and the thrills. Freelancers need a lot of tools. They research and produce the work, they get savvy about markets so they can sell the work, and they secure the contract and hopefully the payment. It's a job. In fact, it's at least three jobs. Thinking of "writing" as what we do with words is such a limited view of our work. I never harbored any illusions that I'd make a living as a poet, but I also had to admit that I thought those who successfully published books had it made. They were somebody while I was still a nobody. Far from it. The work never ends, if you're lucky.

As a poet, correspondence with the visual arts has been an invaluable part of my apprenticeship. At a very practical level, I was able to translate the easel in the fields to an ever-evolving "system" of notebooks and binders for keeping things straight. I didn't want any more napkin drafts. I wanted to be ready when I sensed the constellation taking shape, and I wanted to keep track of my various drafts, journaling, and notes on reading. I evolved various methods for revising poems from handwritten pages in notebooks to hand-cut ¾ sized pages (over and over) to typed versions in binders, which I then revised more. Once my poetry notebook was two hand-sanded thin boards a friend created for me, taking a break from building his own boat. He oiled the wood by hand to a warm glow. Seeing how devoted Tom was to the materials reminded me of the physicality of writing. I used rings that snapped closed, and so could replace the contents but have a permanent structure. Wanting to save paper—and to avoid the pressure that fine stationary can create to write something "worthy" of such materials— for years I used the back sides of computer paper in my notebook. Wanting to save on disposable pens, I bought my first fountain pen while at Penn State, and ironically once I plunked down $35.00 for a single fine writing instrument, I never lost it. Buy ten in a pack and they were gone in a month. Now I buy recycled sewn classroom copybooks (college ruled, only, please) that I wrap in a book cover given to me by the daughter of an A-bomb survivor I'd written about when I lived in Hiroshima. The material itself forms a network of meaning with echoes of associations from my life.

Despite models in the visual arts and great delight in these tools (and so a greater desire to actually use them), all this concern for a working system still embarrasses me. When I consider it within my own experience,

I know that to honor the unexpected formation of "constellations" and to see work through with the dedication I observed in painters and sculptors requires regularity and practiced habits that encourage me to engage in the work. But whenever I speak of it to others, the shadow of obsession passes over, the specter of being perceived as weird or freakish chills me, and the many mouths of doubts come nibbling asking if my so-called work deserves all this stuff and energy. These are simply the stones the village kids hurled at Cezanne as he lumbered out to paint his beloved Sainte-Victoire mountain. If inspiration was like being struck by lightning, artists need to wander around in thunderstorms and we need some equipment to receive that burst of energy. I don't know a writer who doesn't work out their own beloved system for doing the work and keeping track of the various stages of all the projects.

Levertov, in "A Poet's View," answers these hecklers when she states her belief that "creative gifts confer on those who possess them the obligation to nurture them in a degree proportionate to the strength and demands of the gift (which, paradoxically, cannot be determined unless the opportunity for its development be provided, which may mean sacrifices and imbalances in other areas of life)."

In addition, my early immersion in the working methods of visual artists gave me a way to enjoy paintings and sculpture in ways I never had access to. I'll never forget going to the Rodin Museum in Philly, a tiny, quiet haven that reminds no one of Rocky, but not far from where the famous southpaw ran up the steps. Outside the Rodin Museum, I craned my neck to gaze at all the twisted and twisting figures in *The Gates of Hell*. Inside, each pose in *The Burghers of Calais* carried a distinctive emotion; I was reading a short story in this seemingly static sculpture. The dramatic narrative of the visual arts confirmed for me the revelatory detail, the illuminated moment that suggested whole stories. In this way, the visual arts also brought me back to haiku and the Imagists.

The Work of Reading

Once I landed in Seattle, clutching my Rilke and Levertov, I traveled around with the best guide for this moment in my life. Mark hounded used bookstores like no one I've ever known; he once stared at me dumbfounded amid the piles of an Atlantic Book Warehouse when I agonized over spending a few bucks for a find. "Never," he declared as if he'd just come down the mountain in mystic robes, "never not buy used books!" He showed me Pike Place, where there was not yet a Starbucks, but countless bookstores. There I loaded up on all the black-and-white New Directions editions of Rilke, Levertov, and Gary Snyder I could find.

Having returned to *The Imagist Poem*, Sappho's fragments, and Asian poems, having dabbled in drawing to learn to see, and having dedicated myself to a notebook system that symbolized a commitment to my writing, I was ready for another important lesson. How to read. Of course, I read in college; I had to since it was assigned. Well, I read most of it. And some of that I even read well. Not much, I think now, but a little of my assigned and chosen reading I allowed to measure me, to lift my sights to what's possible. Many writing articles talk about how beginning writers need to discover "their voice," but that's wrong-headed. Not only do most writers have many voices, but we join a chorus, a conversation, an ongoing expedition to the limits of language where it returns into silence and the limits of human experience where mystery lives. An apprentice needs to find traveling companions. In my literature classes, professors urged us to learn the tradition while in creative writing classes workshop leaders urged us to go beyond the past, to make it new. Over and over again, John Haag wrote "Read more" on my poems.

I had always scribbled in the margins of my textbooks, copying what teachers told me passages meant, footnoting ideas. In one Religious Studies course on Paul Tillich, I had to write notes just to keep track of those winding Germanic sentences and abstract philosophical language. That kind of engagement with the text is important—without an active pencil, I'd fall asleep bent over Tillich's *Systematic Theology*—but it can be merely functional. Once I entered my apprenticeship, I began to really take notes. I copied out of books the parts that engaged me. I allowed the words to pass through me, from eye to brain/heart, to hand. Just as food passes through the body, nourishing it as it does, this writing was how I devoured books. I copied examples of language leaping, of pulsating imagery, and of concepts that didn't need to be remembered for an exam but for the formation of my heart. Some are cryptic to me now because of the range of material I was dealing with. I copied words I didn't know ("spritely"), graffiti on an overpass ("I © Sue—#1 Sweetheart"), lyrics I'd heard for years but now stood in relief against the blank wall of radio songs, lines from Rilke's *Book of Hours*, quippy sayings on the back of cars ("I Hate Bumperstickers"), the quote I gave from Levertov's "A Poet's View," long passages from Barry Lopez's book *Arctic Dreams*, pages and pages on artists, and scraps of poems by Theodore Roethke, Stanley Kunitz, Maxine Kumin, and others.

I had no idea how much this was preparing me for graduate school, but I was paying attention to my own experience. Just as a constellation can reveal itself in the flow of everyday experience making the first demand of a potential poem, but only those who obey the demand by stepping into solitude and following the first stumblings of language find their way into a poem, there is a momentary pause in the process of reading. In that hesitation, the tide shifts. No longer are words and ideas coming in, but a response goes out. That interaction of self with self is what I record. It is not merely receiving what I read but gathering ways my thinking and feeling extend along the shore of others' writing. I see it as grateful respect for writers, like me, who articulate truths I have not lived into or only intuited and so they remain inchoate until put into words. This system of copying passages continued through grad school and to this day.

Taking notes on my reading, a process I call scribing, evolved into another working method that I consider essential to any apprenticeship. The method is not important, but the lesson and the practice is. With all the poems workshopped in all the creative writing programs all over the country, only one person in my undergraduate classes and only one in my grad classes ever discussed creating books. I am grateful to Maggie Anderson (who was a visiting poet at Penn State) and to Keith Wilson (who was a visiting poet at BGSU) for the clues they provided, but from their threads, I had to find my own way through the labyrinth of writing books, not just individual poems. All writers have to. Just as I had no idea how helpful my method of scribing would prove to be, I did not set out to learn how to construct a collection. I was simply following my own instincts.

Within weeks of my return from bookstore hunting with Mark in Seattle and my pilgrimage to San Francisco to "meet" Kate and visit City Lights, I moved out of my parents' home, quit my deadening job at the *Cable Guide*, and moved in with two friends. This was about a year after graduating from college, and my apprenticeship was taking real shape now.

Frank and I had gone to high school together, and the two of us knew Christian from our mutual participation in the formation program for the Christian Brothers. Along with as many as forty or so others, we all joined up for retreats throughout our undergraduate years; Christian and Frank went on for a year at the Novitiate. Christian spend those months we shared our Henry Avenue apartment in Philadelphia revising his novel. He made a contract with himself, even as he taught history at a vocational high school for the first time, that he would write for five hours a week. An hour a day, and if he missed a day during the week, he'd make it up on the weekend. He said this was how he drafted the novel the previous year. And he stuck with it. His example, which I witnessed up close, remains a model for me because of the way he accommodated visits from his now-wife, Mary, his teaching obligations, and all the other comings and goings of life, but through it all he stayed true to his commitment to his own work. Since Frank was also teaching, but also finishing a grad program and trying to keep a long-distance relationship going, Christian and I shared many meals together, countless conversations about the writing life (and other topics, of course), and many hours of quiet reading.

I was working as a retreat leader for the Department of Youth Services of the Archdiocese of Philadelphia. Our team created reflection experiences—many of them for one day—for school kids and those preparing to receive a new sacrament, like Confirmation or Holy Eucharist, but also weekend retreats for high school students. The writing life and the religious life may seem opposed, but they share a deep and relevant core. Religious experience and spiritual articulation is an exercise in imagination and metaphor, since what we encounter is literally beyond words, our language inevitably falls short of the ineffable. We traveled all over the metropolitan area in our work, which I loved. Our offices were forty-five minutes north of our apartment, so my commute was the reverse of most. I recall keeping a book on the passenger seat, and at red lights, I'd read a Merwin poem or part of one, holding in my mind as I drove the next stretch some phrasing. I was furnishing the palace of my mind with images and poetic forms.

When my two roommates began researching then applying for graduate programs, I was tempted, but I was still going back and forth about whether I'd study some kind of service/ministry or creative writing. The core may be the same but the expression in any single person's life takes distinct forms. My schizophrenia about how to express my calling was embodied in my visit to both the University of Washington, where I knocked on David Waggoner's door to ask what he meant when he scribbled "sorry to say no" on rejection after rejection from *Poetry Northwest*, and to the Seattle University which had a Pastoral Studies program designed to deepen one's individual faith but also prepare one for community service as well. Not ready for formal education, I opted not to go to grad school but continue my informal apprenticeship instead. We dismantled our apartment, said our farewells, and I moved closer to our Bucks County offices, taking a room in a house in Fort Washington.

There, I unpacked my boxes of books and lined them on my Ikea shelves across from my crate and pine board "desk" and was stunned by how little I could recall from these volumes I knew I'd read. Equipped with a word processer, not a computer, but typewriter that had a 7 line screen and some memory—something line 12 pages—I embarked on a project to rectify this forgetting. I began writing my impressions of a collection once I'd read it. I included my questions and confusions, since these were like formal journal entries. I started with books I'd read before but couldn't conjure any of the themes. Of Sharon Olds I wrote, "It's not that I don't like these poems...I feel incomplete, though." Commenting on Merwin's *The Drunk in the Furnace* I admitted that at Penn State, where I first began reading his work, I found the poems beautiful but I didn't understand them, so in this period I started again with the Copper Canyon edition of *The First Four Books*. "Finishing them, I felt as if I should have done my homework more in high school and I had lots of reading to do just to see if I got the gist of these poems. Then came *The Drunk in the Furnace*." I've experienced such breakthroughs since with T.S. Eliot's work, which I likewise read enjoying the music but finding the sense elusive, and some of Pound's work. John Haag was right, the more I read, the more I was prepared to read better. I wrote these comments about Anna Akhmatova (D.M. Thomas translation), Gary Snyder (both a book I'd read before and a new one), Pablo Neruda, Mary Oliver, and others I continue to read and learn from, including Carolyn Forché.

I'd read Forché's memoir of her work in El Salvador while in Maggie Anderson's class, but without making the connection I picked up *The Country Between Us* for $1.98 (in hardcover) at Atlantic Book Warehouse mostly because it was a hardcover collection of poems for less than two bucks. In my post-reading typed reflection, not only do I explain what I liked about the poems, but I could connect images across poems and see how they spoke to each other. I was learning to see not only how individual poems are constructed but also how collections are created. Is it Frost who said that if there are 24 poems in a book, the collection itself is the 25th poem.

Through graduate school I continued to jot these reflections, but soon I was directing them toward other readers, and thus began writing book reviews. It was only after earning my MFA and after volunteering in Hiroshima for two and a half years that this practice of reflecting on whole books revealed the structure of a collection. I reviewed John Balaban's selected poems and could see how the poet's selection of work, the grouping into sections, and the sequence within them all composed meaning just as the images, rhythms, lineation did for a poem. Maybe it was the fact that I was familiar with his work and knew how he changed the sequence that heightened my awareness. Nevertheless, the process of reading daringly and writing about others' collections made important principles and structures settle into place. It would be years still before I could use that recognition since knowledge precedes skill, but I believe I learned it from the inside out, beginning with a practice of typing up a few pages after reading a book I enjoyed. What begins in delight ends in wisdom.

Open Mic and Closed Audience
Through reading I was able to discover my own lineage in the tradition of American poetry, if I have one. While *The Imagist Poem* was a fine textbook

for classes, it was only later that I sensed how the concerns of those Modernists melded with my own interest in the visual arts. And it was only by reading widely, attentively, and reflectively that I saw the connections from Pound and Asian poetry to Gary Snyder and Kenneth Rexroth, from William Carlos Williams to Levertov (and countless others, of course), and from Robert Bly and James Wright so-called Deep Image and surrealism. Forche and Levertov led me to Akhmatova and Neruda who led me to Bly and Wright, and so on. Perhaps I could have saved lots of time by reading a single book that traced these influences—which I have done since then— but discovering it myself was not merely knowledge but identity. I felt welcomed into the community, and I felt some responsibility. To what? For what? I'm still not sure I can articulate. The experience of finding in these people's work impulses and commitments that mirrored my own was more personally affirming than simply knowing what those artistic concerns were.

An apprentice situates himself or herself not only relation to the world and to the structures of experience but also in relation to the community of culture. Art, like the idea of the "communion of saints" I grew up with in my Catholic imagination, helps us transcend time and geography to discover kinship with strangers from other eras, countries, and cultures. These are my people. In this company, I am not *strange* or *weird*, as I sometimes felt even in my supportive and loving family.

Likewise, beginning artists of all kinds need to wrestle with their relationship to their contemporaries. Who is my community now? Do I have an audience? Just as I waited to take creative writing classes until I had learned some literary history, I did not launch into giving poetry readings. This was before slams, "spoken word artists," and other contemporary ways poetry fills the air with the music of the human voice. Mostly there were open mics or reading series with a featured poet, followed by an open mic. Just as I didn't feel ready for formal education for years after graduating from Penn State, I felt I was not ready to take to the podium, and so my first experience reading a poem in public came after a long period of preparing.

Even though I was an English major all four years, I don't recall a very many poetry readings in that time. There were rumors that coffeehouse-style events were once held, and professors and students read and sang, but that era apparently was over and the generation of the MFA with its grad readings and visiting writers had not yet arrived. One event was held in the loungy English Department mailroom. John Haag, with his white hair and bold moustache, sat at the edge of a counter by the cubbies, urging on another reader but never resorting to the tyrannies of a sign-up sheet. I still have an image of a poem by one of my profs from my very first term about waking "still webbed with dream." It was my first vivid experience of hearing a poem that became fully present within me—imagery full figured in my imagination, a concept that was clinched in the ending. I asked for a copy. Sensing something of a connection, I asked Edgar Knapp about his composing process. His response was inexplicable; he said he no longer wrote poems. In my adolescent mind, being a poet was permanent, like being male or Black or married.

The other event was hosted by grad students in my junior or senior year (1985 or 86), and it involved an actual podium, a microphone, and a clipboard for potential readers. I did sign up to read a couple of my own pieces; gratefully, my spiritual advisor from the Christian Brothers was in town, and his support enabled me to lift my tiny, shaking voice to an audible level. But my dominant impression of this formal event was that there was an in-group. Not only was I not in that circle, but part of me did not want to get too close even to the periphery. This was not my community. It seemed that there was too much self-congratulation, use of poetry to show off the writer's erudition, and lots of witty mockery that no one escaped except those whose own wit formed a cool protective bubble. There wasn't even the cloying self-expression of sincere feeling so common in open mic readings I've experienced since then. Well, if I leave my contribution out of it.

Readings were important, though, because the work, which has been labored over in solitude and over so much time, can directly and instantaneously encounter readers, who nod, smile, or say *hmm*. It is communal and dynamic. In an early workshop, I met a fellow student named John Fagan, whose poems at the time completely put me off. "Ziggurat Poems," a classmate called John's cool constructions full of mythologies none of us were familiar with. But John himself was open and authentic, and he believed that poetry was a means of heart-felt communion. He told me that he'd held living room readings, inviting friends to his own apartment for an evening of refreshment and then he'd read. Following his example, I tried one. I used my awkward skills at calligraphy to make invitations, set up chairs, put on music, and read. Frankly, I don't know how it came off, but I never hosted another. Was it because it requires a more forceful promotion of one's self and one's work? Was it because I got negative or (even worse) lukewarm feedback? I know I felt too self-serving, but I still feel that when I encourage people to buy my books. Nevertheless, I love giving readings and knew I had to learn how to do it well.

In the years after Penn State, reading *Writers Digest* with its guidance that we all understand both our "markets" and their readers, I knew I needed to figure out this whole reading/self-promotion thing. I need to state as clearly as I can that I haven't yet. However, in 2005 I attended a panel at the Association of Writers & Writing Programs (AWP) Conference. Each panelist took on a different aspect of giving good readings, confirming what I had discovered; I even had a few things to contribute to the discussion that followed. It made me realize that one component of my apprenticeship was over. Between my living room reading and this affirmation from the community, though, were all kinds of events, one at a bar with a line of men's backs steeling themselves against our words, coffee house readings with espresso machines whining away constantly, one in a bookstore where the host used a stopwatch and cut off readers mid-sentence when their time was up, quite a few where the featured reader was given a free cup of coffee and whatever money listeners put into the hat or basket or cigar box (once a friend put his Visa card in for me), and countless open readings where most in the audience were flipping through their own folders just biding time until their five minutes at the mic.

Living on the fringes of the metro sprawl of Philadelphia, I thought there would be readings galore, but I had to search them out. Formal events—like W.D. Snodgrass at some college or Robert Hass somewhere in the arts community—were easy enough to find since the sponsoring organization has enough money to pay such a big name (in poetry, anyway) so they typically advertised. Listings in the classifieds helped. Finding a seat at these headliner events was sometimes the challenge. I remember listening to Robert Creeley clutching my knees in a hallway, catching his voice through the open door but not catching many of his poems.

The informal readings were a little trickier. I did find one in a used bookstore that took me hours to get to, in a neighborhood I never returned to. I also found some at a bar, at an off-hour, so it didn't interfere with an actual crowd. Finding these events required networking, a process of knowing people and their concerns so that they can inform you of upcoming readings or introduce you to people you should know or give you the skinny on how to get on the list as a featured reader. Since I don't network well, this didn't happen for me. I attend readings, listen appreciatively, and leave. It's such a personal experience for me. Plus, some people's style of networking involves a great deal of egoism. It's not mutual; it's more take-and-take. Some writers are always on the make—some trying to score someone to sleep with and some trying to score their next reading, publication, or residency. To be more successful at networking, I'd have to develop more tolerance for this part of the dynamic the po-biz—and work through it so I can arrive at the more truly communal aspect. It's alive and well, and I glimpsed it even then in the selfless work of the organizers, even the grizzled guy with the stopwatch. No one's getting paid and no one's getting famous.

Still, most of what I learned was a kind of negative space, what-not-to-do. Poet after poet showing off. Look at me, listen to me! Aren't I clever? Aren't I sensitive? Poem after poem that are really sermons, an attempt to convert. Christian, Wiccan, devoted atheism, and every other version of religious belief, of course, but also exhortations to convert us to some version of Earth-loving Hugabuggie or from the High Church of Consumerism or any number of political positions. Long Whitmanesque lists of grievances and offenses.

Conviction to a world-view, a vision of systems and relations, is not the problem, though these readings did feel far longer than their allotted time. The real problem is they assumed a great deal about the "you" or "us" in the poem. And that set the speaker/poet up as the expert, the priest, the righteous one laying out "our" error or "the truth." A self-contained world. If the reader/listener already lives inside the worldview, all is well, but if not, the poem doesn't convince, it bullies. This problem mirrors the personally self-absorbed work. Others have named and analyzed the pervasive experience of immature writers who spill their guts or "share" their anguish and angst, so there's no need to recount those experiences. Again, listening to evening after evening of these kinds of poems formed in me an important influence to wrestle with. There is value in honoring individual struggles and our common humanity. It's an exercise in empathy. But poetry can do more. It can create community. Still, these readings raised good questions to pose for myself. It was valuable. It's one thing to realize which influences to avoid, but how do we know which influences to follow? How do we learn the direction we need to go? If my poems were not going to be conclusions articulated, what could they be?

As an audience member myself, what do I *want* when I attend a reading? What do I hope for? What do I carry away from a good reading? At a practical level, witnessing the trembling papers distract even the reader or leaning closer and closer to just catch a few words of nervous poets who whisper or can't direct their voice toward the mic taught me what to avoid when I got my chance in front of the folding chairs. I had to learn to expect that nervous energy and make use of it. I learned to start with a poem I'm familiar with, one I like and know well enough not to rely on the page too much. Beginning with other people's poems helps me set the bar higher, to name what I aspire to, and so to keep me humble and focus on poetry, not on me. Overly-theatrical readers who came off insincere showed me that style is important but must enhance the drama and intensity of the language, not exceed it. This returned me again and again to the voice in the poem. Beyond typical amateur mistakes, feeling the aimlessness of a famous poet flipping through his book while applying Chapstick as he decided what will happen next made me seek to make a reading a whole, a complete experience. Excellent readings showed me that they could be more than a random set of poems, just as a collection could. If we are to actually give *a* reading, we could use the selection, order, thematic development, and even the patter between poems can create a whole composition. I think of it like a concert: don't musical artists put a great deal of effort into the playlist and rehearsals? Why not poets? Even jam bands and jazz ensembles practice their solos and improvisations.

Nearly twenty years after setting up that crate-and-board desk in my parent's basement, in 2005, not only did I attend the AWP panel on readings, but that year I was also the featured reader at a local poetry festival. In the audience, kids and their proud parents waited for their prizes in the awards ceremony that followed my reading. Other community members and poetry lovers filled out the room. Suppressing my desire to hog the mic (which is considerable), I knew that most listeners were not there to hear me, but they had a significant experience with poetry. Keeping audience in mind, I selected work that was largely narrative, mixing ones about my time in the Cub Scouts and other childhood experiences with a greenhouse poem by Theodore Roethke, Robert Hayden's perfect "Those Winter Sundays," and other "covers." I didn't realize it at the time, but this reading gave me the opportunity to put into action many the principles and structures I'd been developing all through my twenty year apprenticeship.

Formal, Ongoing Apprenticeships

Eventually, I did apply to MFA programs, and was rejected by most. Or if accepted, I was not granted an assistantship, but I was not willing to go into debt for a degree in fine arts. Bowling Green State University accepted me and paid for my schooling. After three years out of school and into my informal apprenticeship, I was ready. I had a system for drafting and revising my work, for keeping track of submissions, and for reflecting on my reading. I was eager to explore styles and voices, traditions and lineages within the long history of poetry, to widen my timeless community.

While at BGSU, I learned from my fellow candidates as I took their influences and intentions seriously, trying their techniques and taking what I could from my many failures. I attended the grad readings in Prout Chapel religiously. We organized a reading series at Grounds for Thought, a bookstore and coffee shop in town.

I am still grateful for several great influences during that time. Michael Mott, who led my first grad workshop, invited us to examine poems from the intention of the writer. Michael also oversaw my thesis, and despite nursing his dying wife, he honored my work by penciling suggestions on draft after draft. Another important influence was Keith Wilson, a visiting writer, who brought the living poetic of the Objectivists together with a mysticism that was itself luminous and had no need to convert others to. The third major influence was working on the *Mid-American Review* with Ken Letko, John Bradley, George Looney, and many, many others.

At the *Mid-Am*, individual readers would evaluate the submissions, and if two said no, it was packed back in its SASE. For those with enough yeses, we'd gather as an editorial team, read them aloud, and discuss each poem. Passionate, ranging discussions. We honored the work. Even the proofreading respected the work. Once the proof pages were ready, we gathered in pairs, one reading from the writer's manuscript and the other looking at the proofs. We read each comma, all the capital letters, and every open-quote, close-quote. I am grateful for this formal stage in my apprenticeship and for the friendships that continue. My spouse and I left Bowling Green to become volunteers in Hiroshima and then we moved back to the States and eventually I become a community college faculty member.

My first and second books came out within a few months of each other, more than fifteen years after completing my MFA. Each cover is graced by artwork by people I know. Each collection has been praised for its haiku-like imagery, the long fulfillment of effort and discipline, of intuition and guesswork, of thousands of bad poems (hopefully learned from), and of the assistance of so many people despite there only being one name on the cover. By the time the collections were tangible objects in the world, some poems were decades old, and I was already working on new books.

All art enjoys a vast history as well as a vast interiority within each maker, so the work goes on. To remind myself of this truth, above my desk I display a quote by Theodore Roethke. I now understand it at a level I couldn't twenty years ago. "Eternal apprenticeship is the life of the true poet." Whether any one of us is a "true poet" or not may be up to others to decide, but I am committed to going on with my apprenticeship, nonetheless, a nobody among nobodies.

USEFUL POETRY WEB SITES

Poetryfoundation.org

Poemhunter.com

Poets.org

Poetrysociety.org

Poetry180 (www.loc.gov/poetry/180)

Versedaily.org

Poems.com

Poetseers.org

Poetryarchive.org

Fishousepoems.org

Librivox.org

Mptmagazine.com

Poem.org

Poetry.com

On-line or partially on-line journals, such as
  Poetry International, h_ngm_n, Mojo, and many more

CREDITS

CONTRIBUTORS

Anderson (Victoria) has been a three-time recipient of Illinois Arts Council grants, and has published her work in numerous periodicals including *Gulf Coast*, *Mississippi Review*, *New South*, and *Agni*, among others. Her first book, *This Country or That*, was the winner of the Mid-America Press Writing award. Her current book, *Vorticity*, was published by Mammoth Press earlier this year. She lives with a man she loves and three aging cats in Chicago. She received her doctorate at Binghamton University and currently teaches poetry and writing at Loyola University Chicago, where she also directs the Writing Program.

Beatty (Jan) is the author of four poetry collections: *The Switching/Yard*, *Red Sugar*, *Boneshaker*, and *Mad River*, winner of the Agnes Lynch Starrett Poetry Prize. She is the recipient of the Creative Achievement Award in Literature from the Heinz Foundation, the Pablo Neruda Prize for Poetry, two fellowships from the Pennsylvania Council on the Arts, and inclusion in *The Best American Poetry 2013*, among other honors. Beatty is cohost and producer of Prosody, a weekly radio program on NPR-affiliate WESA-FM featuring the work of national writers. She is the director of the creative writing program at Carlow University.

Liberal Arts Research Professor of English and Women's Studies at Penn State, **Robin Becker** has published five books in the Pitt Poetry Series, most recently *Tiger Heron*, in 2014. Becker writes the column "Field Notes" for the Women's Review of Books where she serves as Contributing and Poetry Editor. During the 2010-2011 academic year, she traveled Pennsylvania as the Penn State Laureate. Becker has received fellowships from the Massachusetts Cultural Council, the National Endowment for the Arts, and the Bunting Institute at Harvard.

A native of South Carolina, **Bowers's (Cathy Smith)** collections of poetry include *The Love That Ended Yesterday in Texas* (1992), *Traveling in Time of Danger* (1999), *A Book of Minutes* (2004), *The Candle I Hold Up to See You*

(2009), and *Like Shining from Shook Foil* (2010). Press 53 has released *The Collected Poems of Cathy Smith Bowers* in 2014. For many years the poet-in-residence at Queens University of Charlotte, Bowers currently teaches in the low-residency MFA program at Queens, as well as at Wofford College. From 2010 to 2012, she was poet laureate of North Carolina.

Carpathios (Neil) is the author of *Playground of Flesh* (Main Street Rag, 2006), *At the Axis of Imponderables* (winner of the Quercus Review Press Book Award, 2007), and *Beyond the Bones* (FutureCycle Press, 2009); editor of *Every River on Earth: Writing from Appalachian Ohio* (Ohio University Press), to be released in fall of 2014; and author of several award-winning chapbooks. His column in *The Portsmouth Daily Times* is called "Let's Talk Poetry," in which he encourages the appreciation of poetry by showcasing work by local poets in the Southern Ohio region. In 2014, he was awarded his third Individual Excellence Award in poetry from the Ohio Arts Council. He is currently Associate Professor of English and Coordinator of Creative Writing at Shawnee State University in Portsmouth, Ohio.

Closson Buck (Paula) is the author of two books of poems, *The Acquiescent Villa* (1998) and *Litanies Near Water* (2008), both from Louisiana State University Press. She has published poems and stories in such journals as *Agni, Denver Quarterly, Gettysburg Review, Laurel Review, Shenandoah,* and *Southern Review* and is a professor of English at Bucknell University.

Dodd (Elizabeth) is Professor of English at Kansas State University, where she teaches creative writing and literature. She is the author of two books of poetry: *Like Memory, Caverns* and *Archetypal Light.* Her latest nonfiction book is *In the Mind's Eye: Essays Across the Animate World.*

Dougherty (Edward) has been teaching developmental and college level writing, literature, and creative writing, at Corning Community College since 1999, and still considers it noble work. His essays have appeared in *Florida English, North American Review, Cincinnati Review,* and other journals. He is the author of 5 chapbooks, the most recent of which is *Backyard Passages*

(FootHills Publishing), and 2 collections of poetry *Pilgrimage to a Ginkgo Tree*, and *Part Darkness, Part Breath*.

Dougherty (Sean Thomas) is the author or editor of thirteen books. They include *All I Ask for Is Longing: Poems 1994- 2014* (2014 BOA Editions) *Scything Grace* (2013 Etruscan Press) *Sasha Sings the Laundry on the Line* (2010 BOA Editions) which was a finalist for Binghamton University's Milton Kessler literary prize for the best book by a poet over 40, the novella *The Blue City* (2008 Marick Press/Wayne State University), and *Broken Hallelujahs* (2007 BOA Editions). His awards include two Pennsylvania Council for the Arts Fellowships, a Fulbright Lectureship to the Balkans, and an appearance in Best American Poetry 2014. He works in a pool hall in Erie, PA, travels extensively for performances, and teaches private students.

Gallaher (John) is the author of three poetry collections, most recently, *Map of the Folded World* (University of Akron Press, 2009). His honors include the 2005 Levis Poetry Prize for his second book, *The Little Book of Guesses* (Four Way Books). His poetry has been published in literary journals and magazines including *Boston Review, Colorado Review, Crazyhorse, Field, jubilat, The Journal, Ploughshares,* and in anthologies including *The Best American Poetry 2008*. He is co-editor of *The Laurel Review* and resides in Maryville, Missouri, where he teaches creative writing and composition courses at Northwest Missouri State University.

Gills (Michael) is author of *Why I Lie: Stories* (University of Nevada Press, 2002), *Go Love: A Novel* (Raw Dog Screaming Press, 2011), *The Death of Bonnie and Clyde and Other Stories* (Texas Review Press, 2012) and *White Indians* (Raw Dog Screaming Press, 2013). He is Associate Professor/ Lecturer at the University of Utah. Gills' collected papers are archived at Martha Blakeney Hodges Special Collections and University Archives, The University of North Carolina at Greensboro. He grows tomatoes in the Wasatch foothills with his wife, daughter, rabbits, chickens and dog, and is mustering strength to teach one of the first year-long novel workshops for undergraduates.

Greenhouse (Melanie) has worked with poets and poetry for over 25 years. She co-founded and directed the Arts Cafe~ Mystic for its first decade bringing internationally known poets to Southeastern CT. The award-winning series is reaching its 20th anniversary. She has worked with a cross-section of generations, from teens to senior citizens, helping them to discover their true subjects. Her program, Gray Dawn Breaking, is in its sixth year using poetry and life experience as a means to enhance memory and cognition in the older individual. Melanie lives and writes on the outskirts of Noank, Connecticut.

Grieneisen (Jeff), an assistant professor of English, literature and creative writing at State College of Florida, earned his MFA from University of New Orleans. MAMMOTH Books published his first book of poetry, *Good Sumacs*, in 2011. He is co-founder and associate editor of the annual literary journal *Florida English*. His critical work includes published scholarship on Ezra Pound, and he co-authored, with his wife Courtney, articles on Edgar Allan Poe for Harold Bloom's *Biocritiques* series (Chelsea House) and *Critical Insights: The Tales of Poe* (EBSCO/Salem). Among many journals and anthologies, his poetry has been published in Portuguese translation in the Brazilian academic journal *Revisto Espaço Acadêmico*. He divides his time between southwest Florida and western Pennsylvania.

Hettich's (Michael) books include *LIKE HAPPINESS* (2010) and *THE ANIMALS BEYOND US* (2011) as well as the chapbook *THE MEASURED BREATHING* (2011). His new book, *SYSTEMS OF VANISHING*, won the 2013 Tampa Review Prize in Poetry and was published in April, 2014. He lives and teaches in Miami.

Heyen (William) is Professor of English/Poet in Residence Emeritus at SUNY Brockport, his undergraduate alma mater. His MA and Ph.D degrees are from Ohio University, and he has been awarded an Honorary Doctorate of Humane Letters by SUNY. A former Senior Fulbright Lecturer in American Literature in Germany, he has won NEA, Guggenheim, American Academy & Institute of Arts & Letters, and other fellowships and awards. His work has appeared in hundreds of anthologies and in magazines including *The New Yorker*, *The Atlantic*, *Harper's*, *American Poetry Review*, *Kenyon Review*, *The Southern Review*. He is the editor or author of more than thirty books including *Noise in the Trees*, an American Library Association Notable Book for 1975; *Crazy Horse in Stillness*, winner of 1997's Small Press Book Award for Poetry; *Shoah Train: Poems*, a Finalist for the 2004 National Book Award; and *A Poetics of Hiroshima*, a Chautauqua Literary & Scientific Circle selection in 2010. Three new books of poetry (*Straight's Suite for Craig Cotter & Frank O'Hara*, *The Football Corporations*, and *Hiroshima Suite*) and the first two volumes of his massive journal (*The Cabin* and *Hannelore*), appeared in 2012 and 2013.

Hogue (Cynthia) has published twelve books, including *Or Consequence* and *When the Water Came: Evacuees of Hurricane Katrina* (interview-poems with photographs), both in 2010; the co-translated *Fortino Sámano (The overflowing of the poem)*, by Virginie Lalucq and Jean-Luc Nancy (Omnidawn 2012), winner of the 2013 Harold Morton Landon Translation Award from the Academy of American Poets; and the co-edited *Innovative Women Poets: An Anthology of Contemporary Poetry and Interviews*. Her eighth collection of poetry is entitled *Revenance* (Red Hen Press, 2014). She is the Maxine and Jonathan Marshall Chair of Modern and Contemporary Poetry at Arizona State University.

Hollander (Andrea) is the author of four full-length poetry collections, most recently *Landscape with Female Figure: New & Selected Poems, 1982 – 2012* (Autumn House Press, 2013), and the editor of *When She Named Fire: An Anthology of Contemporary Poetry by American Women* (Autumn House, 2009). Her many honors include two poetry fellowships from the National Endowment for the Arts, the Nicholas Roerich Poetry Prize, the D. H. Lawrence Fellowship, a Pushcart Prize for prose memoir, and literary fellowships from the arts councils of both Arkansas and Oregon, where she lives now. For 22 years Hollander was the Writer-in-Residence at Lyon College, where she was awarded the Lamar Williamson Prize for Excellence in Teaching. Her website is www.andreahollander.net.

Hughes (Henry) is the author of three collections of poetry, including *Men Holding Eggs,* which received the 2004 Oregon Book Award. He is the editor of the *Everyman's Library* anthologies, *The Art of Angling: Poems about Fishing and Fishing Stories,* and his commentary on new poetry appears regularly in *Harvard Review.* He teaches at Western Oregon University.

Jackson (Richard) teaches at UT-Chattanooga and is a frequent lecturer at the MFA writing seminars at Vermont College, University of Iowa Summer Writers' Festival, Yale Writers Conference, and the Prague Summer Program. He is the author of eleven books of poems most recently, *Out of Place,* and *Resonance* (Eric Hofer Award). His twelfth book, *Retrievals,* is the Maxine Kumin Award winner to be published in 2015. He has also published two books of translations, *Last Voyage: The Poems of Giovanni Pascoli* from Italian (2010) and Alexandar Persolja's *Journey of the Sun* from Slovene (2008). He is also the author of two critical books, *Acts of Mind: Conversations with American Poets* (Choice Award) and *Dismantling Time in Contemporary Poetry* (Agee Award Winner), and has edited two anthologies of Slovene poetry, as well as the journal *Poetry Miscellany.* His work has been translated into fifteen languages including a Spanish edition of *Resonance* to appear in Barcelona in 2014, and has appeared in *The Best American Poems,* among other collections. He has been awarded the *Order of Freedom Medal* by the President of Slovenia for literary and humanitarian work in the Balkans, and has been named a Guggenheim Fellow, Fulbright Fellow, Witter-Bynner Fellow, NEA fellow, NEH Fellow, and has lectured and given readings at dozens of universities and conferences here and abroad. In 2009 he won the AWP George Garret National Award for Teaching and Arts Advocacy. His web page is at http://members.authorsguild.net/svobodni/

James (Mike) has been widely published in magazines throughout the country. He has published seven poetry collections. *Elegy in Reverse* (2014, Aldrich Press) and *Past Due Notices: Poems 1991-2011* (2012, Main Street Rag) are his most recent. He also serves as the associate editor of *The Kentucky Review* and is the publisher, with his wife Diane, of Yellow Pepper

Press, a small poetry broadside press. After years spent in South Carolina, Missouri and Pennsylvania he now lives in Douglasville, Georgia with his wife and five children.

Kaminsky (Ilya) was born in Odessa, former Soviet Union in 1977, and arrived to the United States in 1993, when his family was granted asylum by the American government. Ilya is the author of *Dancing In Odessa* (Tupelo Press, 2004), which won the Whiting Writer's Award, the American Academy of Arts and Letters' Metcalf Award, the Dorset Prize, the Ruth Lilly Fellowship given annually by *Poetry* magazine. *Dancing In Odessa* was also named Best Poetry Book of the Year 2004 by *ForeWord Magazine*. In 2008, Kaminsky was awarded Lannan Foundation's Literary Fellowship. Poems from his new manuscript, *Deaf Republic*, were awarded *Poetry* magazine's Levinson Prize and the Pushcart Prize. His anthology of 20th century poetry in translation, *Ecco Anthology of International Poetry*, was published by Harper Collins in March, 2010. His poems have been translated into numerous langauges and his books have been published in Holland, Russia, France, Spain. Another translation is forthcoming in China, where his poetry was awarded the Yinchuan International Poetry Prize. Kaminsky has worked as a law clerk for San Francisco Legal Aid and the National Immigration Law Center. Currently, he teaches English and Comparative Literature at San Diego State University.

Kinsley (Robert) is the author of two collections, *Endangered Species* and *Field Stones*, both from Orchises Press. His poems have appeared in various magazines and he is a past recipient of an Ohio Arts Council Individual Artist Award. He is recently retired from Ohio University.

Kitson (Herb), Professor of English, teaches classes in developmental English, freshman composition, and literature at the University of Pittsburgh at Titusville, where he also works six hours per week in the Learning Center. His poetry has appeared in such publications as *The Atlanta Review*, *The Green Mountains Review*, *The New York Quarterly*, *Poetry East*, and *Yankee*.

Knorr (Jeff) is the current Poet Laureate of Sacramento. He is the author of the three books of poetry, *The Third Body* (Cherry Grove Collections), *Keeper* (Mammoth Books), and *Standing Up to the Day* (Pecan Grove Press). His other works include *Mooring Against the Tide: Writing Poetry and Fiction* (Prentice Hall); the anthology, *A Writer's Country* (Prentice Hall); and *The River Sings: An Introduction to Poetry* (Prentice Hall). His poetry and essays have appeared in numerous literary journals and anthologies including *Chelsea, Connecticut Review, The Journal, North American Review, Red Rock Review, Barrow Street,* and *Like Thunder: Poets Respond to Violence in America* (University of Iowa). Jeff Knorr lives in Sacramento, California and is Professor of literature and creative writing at Sacramento City College.

Koestenbaum (Phyllis) is the author of eight poetry books and chapbooks, among them *oh I can't she says, Criminal Sonnets* and, most recently, *Doris Day and Kitschy Melodies,* a collection of prose poems. Her work has been published in numerous anthologies, textbooks and journals, including in two volumes of *The Best American Poetry.* Her essay, "The Secret Climate the Year I Stopped Writing," published in *The Massachusetts Review,* was listed as one of the Notable Essays of 2007 in *The Best American Essays.* A recipient of fellowships from the National Endowment for the Arts, the California Arts Council and the Djerassi Foundation, she was until recently a Senior Scholar at Stanford University's Clayman Institute for Gender Research.

LaFemina (Gerry) is the author of thirteen books of poetry, prose poetry and prose, including most recently *Little Heretic* (2014, poems, Stephen F. Austin University Press) and *Clamor* (2013, novel, Codorus Press). He directs the Center for Creative Writing at Frostburg State University where he is also an Associate Professor of English. He divides his time between Maryland and New York and serves as Executive Director of Poets at Work.

Levin's (Harriet) debut book of poem, *The Christmas Show* (Beacon Press) was chosen by Eavan Boland for the Barnard New Women Poets Prize and also received the Alice Fay di Castagnola Award from the Poetry Society of America. Her second book, *Girl in Cap and Gown* (Mammoth Books) was a National Poetry Series finalist. Her poems and short stories have appeared in *Antioch Review, Cimarron Review, Harvard Review, Iowa Review, Kenyon Review, Ploughshares, Prairie Schooner* and *Smart Set*, among other journals. She has recently completed a novel about a Lost Boy of Sudan based on her work reuniting Lost Boys of Sudan with their mothers living abroad. She teaches creative writing at Drexel University where she is director of the Certificate Program in Writing and Publishing.

Maddox (Marjorie) is Director of Creative Writing and Professor of English at Lock Haven University. She has published nine collections of poetry—including *Local News from Someplace Else*, a 2013 ebook *of Perpendicular As I* (1994 Sandstone Book Award), and *Transplant, Transport, Transubstantiation* (2004 Yellowglen Prize)—as well as over 450 poems, stories, and essays in journals and anthologies. She is co-editor *of Common Wealth: Contemporary Poets on Pennsylvania* and has two children's books, *A Crossing of Zebras: Animal Packs in Poetry* and *Rules of the Game: Baseball Poems* . Her numerous honors include Cornell University's Sage Graduate Fellowship for an MFA, Cornell's Chasen Award, the 2000 Paumanok Poetry Award, an Academy of American Poets Prize, the *Seattle Review's* Bentley Prize for Poetry, a Bread Loaf Scholarship, Pushcart Prize nominations in both poetry and fiction, and Lock Haven University's 2012 Honors Professor of the Year. She is the great grandniece of baseball legend Branch Rickey, the general manager of the Brooklyn Dodgers who helped break the color barrier by signing Jackie Robinson. For more information, see www.marjoriemaddox.com

Margolis (Gary), Ph.D, is Emeritus Executive Director of College Mental Health Services and Associate Professor of English and American Literatures (part-time) at Middlebury College. He has been a Robert Frost and Arthur Vining Davis Fellow and has taught at the University of Tennessee, Vermont and Bread Loaf Writers' Conferences. His new book, *Raking the Winter Leaves: New and Selected Poems* is nominated for the 2013 Pulitzer Prize.

Mathews (Sebastian) is the author of a memoir, two books of poems and an art catalogue on the early collage works of Ray Johnson. He lives with his family in Asheville, North Carolina. He's currently working on a novel.

McClanahan (Rebecca) has published ten books, most recently *The Tribal Knot: A Memoir of Family, Community, and a Century of Change.* The recipient of the Wood Prize from *Poetry*, the Glasgow prize in nonfiction, and fellowships from New York Foundation for the Arts and the North Carolina Arts Council, she teaches in the MFA programs of Queens University (Charlotte) and Rainier Writing Workshop at Pacific Lutheran.

Minar (Scott) is the author of *The Body's Fire* (Clarellen 2002) and *The Palace of Reasons* (MAMMOTH Books 2006); coauthor (with Edward Dougherty) of *Exercises for Poets: Double Bloom* (Pearson/Prentice Hall 2006); editor of *The Working Poet: 75 Writing Exercises and a Poetry Anthology* (Autumn House 2009) and this edition, *The Working Poet II: 50 Writing Exercises and a Poetry Anthology* (MAMMOTH Books 2014). His poetry has appeared in *The Paris Review, Poetry International, Crazyhorse, The Georgia Review, Ninth Letter, TickleAce, West Branch, The Laurel Review, Verse Daily,* and other journals and anthologies in the U.S. and Canada. He has taught at Memorial University of Newfoundland, Antioch College, Bowling Green State University, Ohio University, and Elmira College. He is currently Professor of English at Ohio University Lancaster.

Mirskin (Jerry) won the MAMMOTH Books Poetry Prize for his first collection, *Picture a Gate Hanging Open and Let that Gate be the Sun. Crepuscular Non Driveway* is his third full-length collection. His second collection, *In Flagrante Delicto* was also published by MAMMOTH. He was born in the Bronx, and has lived in California, Wisconsin and Maine. He has worked as a herdsman on a dairy farm, as a carpenter, and as a New York State Poet-in-the-Schools. He has published widely in literary journals and anthologies. He is currently an Associate Professor at Ithaca College and lives in Ithaca, New York, with his wife, Wendy Dann, a playwright and theatrical director. He has a son, Noah.

Moncrieff (Scott) is Professor of English at Andrews University. He is the author of *Screen Deep* (2008), a collection of essays on popular culture. He loves reading, writing, and teaching poetry because you never know when the next magical combination of words will come around the corner. For relaxation, he plays upright bass in a local jazz trio.

Muir (Sharona) writing has received the National Endowment for the Arts Fellowship; the Alfred Hodder Fellowship from Princeton University; two Ohio Arts Council Fellowships; the Memorial Foundation for Jewish Culture Fellowship; the Bernard F. Connors Prize, and other awards. She is the author of four books: *Invisible Beasts: Tales of the Animals that Go Unseen Among Us*, Bellevue Literary Press; *The Book of Telling: Tracing the Secrets of My Father's Lives*, Random House/Schocken Books; *The Artificial Paradise: Science Fiction And American Reality*, in the series "Studies in Literature and Science" from University of Michigan Press; and *During Ceasefire*, a collection of poetry from Harper & Row. She is represented by the Georges Borchardt Literary Agency, 136 East 57th Street, New York, NY 10022. Her poetry and prose have been published in numerous journals including *Granta*, *The Paris Review*, *Stand*, *Orion*, *ISLE*, *Nautilus*, *The Yale Review*, *Harvard Magazine*, *Virginia Quarterly Review*, *Prairie Schooner*, *The Kenyon Review*, *The Antioch Review*, *Parnassus*, *Michigan Quarterly Review*, *Partisan Review*, *Denver Quarterly*, *Missouri Review*, and *The Jerusalem Report*. She has been a writer-in-residence at the Fine Arts Work Center in Provincetown, the Djerassi Resident Artists Program, and Mishkenot Sha'ananim in Jerusalem. She holds a Ph.D. in Modern Thought and Literature from Stanford University, an M.A. in Creative Writing and English from Boston University, and an A.B. in Comparative Literature from Princeton University. She is currently Professor of Creative Writing and English at Bowling Green State University.

Murphy (Erin) is the author of six books of poetry, most recently *Ancilla* (Lamar University Press, 2014), and is co-editor of *Making Poems: Forty Poems with Commentary by the Poets* (SUNY Press, 2010). Her works have been published in numerous journals and anthologies and featured on Garrison Keillor's *The Writer's Almanac*. She teaches English at Penn State Altoona. Website: erin-murphy.com

Pushcart Prize recipient and Founding Editor of Four Way Books, **Dzvinia Orlowsky** is the author of five poetry collections published by Carnegie Mellon University Press including her most recent, *Silvertone*. Her first collection, A *Handful of Bees*, was reprinted in 2008 as a Carnegie Mellon University Classic Contemporary. Dzvinia's poetry and translations have appeared in numerous magazines and anthologies including *A Map of Hope: An International Literary Anthology; From Three Worlds: New Writing from Ukraine*; and *A Hundred Years of Youth: A Bilingual Anthology of 20th Century Ukrainian Poetry*. Her translation from the Ukrainian of Alexander Dovzhenko's novella, *The Enchanted Desna*, was published by House Between Water press in 2006. Her co-translation with Jeff Friedman from the Polish of Mieczysław Jastrun's *Memorials* is going to be published later this year or early in 2015 by Dialogos. Dzvinia teaches at the Solstice Low-Residency MFA Program of Creative Writing of Pine Manor College and as Special Lecturer at Providence College.

Pearson (Pen) is a professor of English at Northern State University in Aberdeen, South Dakota. Her publications include a chapbook, Trespass to Chattel (Atomic Press, 2009) and a full-length collection of poems, *Poetry as Liturgy* (Mellen Press, 2010). Her current project is a biographical novel of modernist British poet Charlotte Mew.

Pineda (Jon) is the author of the poetry collections THE TRANSLATOR'S DIARY, winner of the Green Rose Prize, and BIRTHMARK, winner of the Crab Orchard Award Series in Poetry Open Competition. His memoir SLEEP IN ME was a Barnes & Noble Discover Great New Writers selection, and his debut novel APOLOGY won the 2013 Milkweed National Fiction Prize. He lives in Virginia with his family and teaches creative writing at the University of Mary Washington.

Potter (Eric) is a professor of English at Grove City College where he teaches courses in the humanities, American literature, modern poetry, and creative writing. In addition to scholarly articles and conference presentations, he has published two poetry chapbooks. He lives in western Pennsylvania with his wife and three children.

Raab (Lawrence) is the author of seven collections of poems, most recently *The History of Forgetting* (Penguin, 2009) and *A Cup of Water Turns into a Rose*, a long poem published as a chapbook by Adastra Press (2012). He teaches literature and writing at Williams College.

Rich (Susan) is the author of four collections of poetry, including *Cloud Pharmacy, The Alchemist's Kitchen* (named a finalist for the Foreword Prize and the Washington State Book Award), *Cures Include Travel*, and *The Cartographer's Tongue / Poems of the World* which won the PEN USA Award for Poetry and the Peace Corps Writers Award. She has received awards and fellowships from Artist Trust, CityArtists, 4Culture, The Times Literary Supplement of London, Peace Corps Writers and the Fulbright Foundation. Rich's poems have appeared in *The Harvard Review, New England Review, and the Southern Review.* Rich has traveled to Bosnia Herzegovina, South Africa, and the West Bank as a human rights activist and electoral supervisor. She has worked as a PeaceCorps Volunteer, a Program Coordinator for Amnesty International, and now teaches English and film studies at Highline Community College. Her featured appearances include the Cuirt Literary Festival in Galway, Ireland; Seattle Arts and Lectures, Seattle, WA; and the University of Sarajevo, Bosnia. Recent poems have been published in *the Harvard Review, Gettysburg Review, Poetry International, The Southern Review* and the *New England Review.* Born and educated in Massachusetts, with advanced degrees from Harvard University and the University of Oregon, Susan now makes her home in Seattle, WA.

Rosenberg (Liz) is the author of 4 novels, 5 books of poems and more than 20 award winning books for children. She teaches English and creative

328 • THE WORKING POET

writing at Binghamton University and was a 2014 Fulbright Fellow in North Ireland.

Rosko's (Emily) two poetry collections are *Prop Rockery*, awarded the 2011 Akron Poetry Prize, and *Raw Goods Inventory*, an Iowa Poetry Prize winner in 2005. She is editor of *A Broken Thing: Poets on the Line* (University of Iowa Press, 2011), and poetry editor for *Crazyhorse*. She is assistant professor of English and Creative Writing at the College of Charleston.

Sajé's (Natasha) first book of poems, *Red Under the Skin* (Pittsburgh, 1994), won the Agnes Lynch Starrett Prize, and her second collection, *Bend* (Tupelo, 2004), was given the Utah Book Award in Poetry. Her third book of poems, *Vivarium*, is just out from Tupelo. Her book of essays *Windows and Doors: A Poet Reads Literary Theory* will be published by the University of Michigan Press in 2014. She teaches at Westminster College in Salt Lake City and in the Vermont College of Fine Arts MFA program.

In addition to *That hum to go by* (Mammoth books, 2012), **Schiff (Jeff)** is the author of *Mixed Diction, Burro Heart, The Rats of Patzcuaro, The Homily of Infinitude, Anywhere in this Country,* and *Resources for Writing About Literature*. His work has appeared internationally in more than eighty periodicals, including *The Alembic, Grand Street, The Ohio Review, Poet & Critic, The Louisville Review, Tendril, Pembroke Magazine, Carolina Review, Chicago Review, Hawaii Review, Southern Humanities Review, River City, Indiana Review, Willow Springs,* and *The Southwest Review.* He has been a member of the English faculty at Columbia College Chicago since 1987.

Silano (Martha) is the author of four books of poetry, including *The Little Office of the Immaculate Conception* (2011) and *Reckless Lovely* (2014), both from Saturnalia Books. She is co-editor, with Kelli Russell Agodon, of *The Daily Poet: Day-By-Day Prompts for Your Writing Practice* (TwoSylvias 2013). Martha edits *Crab Creek Review* and teaches at Bellevue College.

Stigall (**John, November 4, 1951 - November 12, 2009**) was an American poet, Associate Professor of English, and poet-in-residence at Chattanooga State Technical Community College. John Stigall received a Bachelors of Arts from the State University of New York at Cortland, and a Master of Arts from the State University of New York at Brockport. It was at Brockport in 1980 that he wrote his Master's thesis: The Morale of Consciousness Wails. After attaining both degrees, he returned to Chattanooga and became Associate Professor of English and poet-in-residence at Chattanooga State Technical Community College. There he founded and became editor of the campus' literary magazine *The Phoenix*. Bill Stifler dedicated the 2001 edition of *The Phoenix* to him. He also received the Outstanding Young Educator Award and other honors while he taught. Towards the end of his professorship, he was asked to read from *Broken Mirrors Reflect the World* at Pennsylvania State University and SUNY; his book, *Subject for Other Conversations*, was subsequently taught at Pennsylvania State University for a brief period. His books include, *In Avant Gardens* (1983) Damballah Press ISBN 0-913649-01-5; *Broken Mirrors Reflect the World* (1990) Damballah Press ISBN 0-913649-05-8; *Schizofrenzy* (1993) Mammoth Books; *Subjects for Other Conversations* (2001) Mammoth Books ISBN 0-9666028-6-2; and Smiling From the Ancestral Face (Incomplete).

Terman (**Philip**) is the author of four collections of poetry: *The House of Sages* (MAMMOTH Books, 1998); *Book of the Unbroken Days* (Mammoth, 2005) and *Rabbis of the Air* (Autumn House Press, 2007), and *The Torah Garden* (Autumn House Press, 2011). His poems and essays have appeared in many journals and anthologies, including *Poetry*, *Georgia Review*, *Kenyon Review*, and *Blood to Remember: American Poets Respond to the Holocaust*. A Professor of English at Clarion University, he is also co-director of the Chautauqua Writers' Festival (writers.ciweb.org/writers-festival).

Vallone (**Antonio**) is an associate professor of English at Penn State DuBois. He also teaches in National University's online MFA program. Editor of *Pennsylvania English* and publisher of MAMMOTH books, his own books are *Golden Carp*, *The Blackbird's Applause*, *Grass Saxophones*, and *Chinese Bats*. Forthcoming are *American Zen* and *Blackberry Alleys: Collected Poems*. He can be reached at avallone@psu.edu.

Webb (Charles Harper) is the author of ten books of poetry, including *Shadow Ball: New and Selected Poems*, and *What Things Are Made Of*, both from University of Pittsburgh Press. Editor of *Stand Up Poetry: An Expanded Anthology*, Webb has received the Morse Prize, Pollak Prize, Saltman Prize, and Kate Tufts Discovery Award, as well as grants from the Whiting and Guggenheim Foundations. He teaches at California State University, Long Beach, where he has served as both Director of Creative Writing and MFA Director.

ACKNOWLEDGEMENTS

My greatest thanks go as always to my wife, the wonderful Roberta Milliken, the best editor and strategic thinker that I know, whose own work ethic humbles all who know her well and inspires me every day to do my best out of the same love of language, teaching, and learning that inspires her; motivates her students; and impels her friends, mentees, and colleagues toward the same. She is the sine qua non of all good things in my life.